Eric Hosking's

BIRDS OF PREY
OF THE WORLD

Kestrels often hover
while scanning for prey,
but here a female takes
advantage of a perch to
scan for large insects
(which feature
commonly in its diet)
passing beneath.

Eric Hosking's
BIRDS OF PREY
OF THE WORLD

Eric and David Hosking
with Jim Flegg

THE STEPHEN GREENE PRESS
Lexington, Massachusetts

Large feet securely
grasping a slippery fish,
the Osprey begins its
meal on a favoured
feeding perch.

For Mark and Simon

Copyright © Eric Hosking, David Hosking, and
Jim Flegg, 1987
All rights reserved

First published in Great Britain in 1987 by
Pelham Books Ltd.
First published in the United States of America in 1988
by The Stephen Greene Press Inc.
Distributed by Viking Penguin Inc., 40 West 23rd Street,
New York, NY 10010

CIP data available

ISBN 0-8289-0653-X

Printed in Italy by Olivotto

Set in Italia Book

CONTENTS

Preface and Acknowledgements   6

1 Birds of Prey: an introduction   9

2 Birds of Prey in Action   17

3 Birds of Prey the World Over   31

4 Family Portraits   41
The family *Cathartidae* – New World Vultures   43
The family *Sagittariidae* – Secretary Bird   46
The family *Accipitridae*   47
  Kites   47
  Honey Buzzards   51
  Hawks   52
    Sparrowhawk *Accipiter nisus*   58
  Harriers   63
  Buzzards   68
  Eagles   79
    Golden Eagle *Aquila chrysaetos*   96
    Bald Eagle *Haliaeetus leucocephalus*   99
    African Fish Eagle *Haliaeetus vocifer*   106
  Old World Vultures   108
The family *Pandionidae* – Osprey   120
The family *Falconidae* – Falcons and Caracaras   125
  Kestrel *Falco tinnunculus*   130
  Peregrine *Falco peregrinus*   135
Australian Birds of Prey   140

5 Conservation   147

6 Falconry   157

7 Birds of Prey of the World
  and their Distribution   165

Further Reading   173

Index   174

PREFACE AND ACKNOWLEDGEMENTS

As always, it gives us great pleasure to acknowledge our sincere thanks to all those who have made it possible for us to produce this book. We devote our lives to taking photographs but we are not authors: we owe a great debt to Dr Jim Flegg for writing such an authoritative text. We envy his ability as a writer and his considerable knowledge of the birds of prey of the world.

Eric was responsible for the photography on the Mountfort Expeditions; he vividly remembers sitting in the hide within 20 feet of an Imperial Eagle's eyrie, in the Coto Donana in Southern Spain. Not only is it extremely rare, but this was probably the first occasion it had ever been portrayed at the nest. Excitement reached fever pitch as the adult was observed flying back to the nest with a rabbit dangling from its talons. There was just a single eaglet, still covered in down and the parent bird began to rip to pieces the prey and gently feed small morsels to the chick. On another occasion on this same trip, we had built a pylon hide by the nest of a Short-toed Eagle. A snake five times the length of the eaglet was given to it by the hen and the seemingly impossible task was filmed of the young swallowing this complete in 35 minutes.

Donald Smith arranged for us to photograph Golden Eagles in Ayrshire. Val Gargett and Peter Steyn took us on a visit to an old hide that had been erected by the nest of a Black Eagle's eyrie in Zimbabwe. They thought we might be interested to see the site. Imagine the thrill when we watched the eaglet that had been fledged for some time suddenly alight on the nest, followed by the cock carrying a Hyrax. He dropped this and the chick mantled over it as the hen arrived. Peter and Val had both spent hundreds of hours watching these eagles, but had never seen all the family together at one time.

Again, we were exceptionally fortunate to meet Jeff Watson while in the Seychelles. He was working on his Ph.D. thesis on the rare Seychelles Kestrel. When Eric asked what chance there was of photographing one, he calmly replied 'No problem'. As this was not during their breeding season, we wondered what he had in mind: it turned out that he knew a place where one roosted every night. At dusk, the Kestrel arrived and took no notice of Jeff and Eric standing within six feet nor did it take any exception to the flash as they took numerous photographs of it.

John Karmali and John Williams both helped us greatly, while working in East Africa; without them we might not have succeeded in getting pictures of some of the vultures, eagles and kites. Not only did they drive us to the right place, but they manoeuvred the car so that we could take the photographs from the window. While staying in Australia, Dr David Hollands invited Eric to use a hide he had erected at bait in the hope of getting pictures of a Wedge-tailed Eagle. Although the Eagle did not arrive, a beautiful Australian Goshawk did. While in Australia David and Molly Trounson drove us to many places and one evening as we were returning to our motel, we saw a Little Eagle perched near the top of a dead tree. The light was poor, it seemed impossible to get a photograph, but by wedging the big 600mm lens and camera firmly against the window frame a few successful results were obtained.

While in Sri Lanka, James Ferguson-Lees

noticed a White-bellied Sea Eagle perched in a tree so we drove slowly towards it and managed to get within photographic range.

Yossi Lesham, of the Society for the Protection of Nature in Israel, and Bill Clark enabled us to portray Steppe Eagles at Eilat; Ofer Bahat and Reuven Yosef acted as our guides during our stay and their keen eyes spotted eagles, kites and other birds for us to photograph.

We must also thank Dr Johan Willgohs, who took us to a White-tailed Eagle's eyrie in Norway; Lars Eric Lindblad, who invited us to go on board the *MS Explorer* and while down in the Falklands we found Striated Caracaras; Margaret Woodward, who took the photograph of the White-tailed Eagle on the island of Rhum, where they are being hand reared and reintroduced to the wild.

To obtain some of the pictures we required for this book David travelled to The Gambia and is most grateful to Eddie Brewer and the staff of the Abuko Nature Reserve for their help, and to Martin and Julie Eccles for providing four types of vulture to photograph. Without Chris White's background information, few subjects would have been recorded on film. During a family holiday in Florida with Martin and Sally Withers, David and Martin were able to find and photograph five new subjects for this book. The one species they did not even see was the unusual Snail Kite, and we would like to thank Gordon Langsbury for letting us use his picture. No book on birds of prey would be complete without a reference to the Bald Eagle. This species has always eluded our cameras in the wild, so we are grateful to David's wife Jean, who runs the Frank Lane Picture Agency, for providing us with these pictures taken by her photographers Steve McCutcheon, Glenn Elison and Mark Newman.

Much as we would have liked all the illustrations for this book to be in the wild, there was just not enough time to be in the right place at the right time and we have included some photographs that were taken in our portable studio. We would like to thank those who welcomed us to their collections: Phillip Glasier and his daughter, Jemima Parry Jones, who is the director of the Falconry Centre at Newent, Glos., both put themselves out in innumerable ways to make sure we got the birds in their best plumages. Phillip even built us a turn-table, on to which we could put a small rock for the bird to perch on, and then with the aid of string turn the bird round to show front, side and back views. Dr Michael Brambell gave us great help at Chester Zoo; Bill Timmis, a real expert aviculturalist, assisted in many ways at Harewood House. Reg Smith at the Hawk Trust permitted us to photograph in his excellent collection. Probably the hardest bird of prey to find in captivity is the Gyrfalcon and we are very grateful to Roger Upton and his son, Mark, for letting us photograph their lovely male.

It is one thing to have the bird in front of you, but quite another to be able to photograph it successfully, so we are more than pleased to thank Barry Taylor and the staff of Olympus Optical Company for their help.

We would like to thank Dick Douglas-Boyd, Publisher of Pelham Books for the enthusiasm and encouragement he gave us, and to all the staff of Pelham who worked so hard to produce this book.

Photographing the birds of prey of the world has given us immense pleasure, great excitement and many thrills, but this grand family is struggling for survival as habitat destruction, pollution and pesticides take their toll. So often a bird of prey is at the end of the food chain and dies as a result of eating animals that have themselves been weakened or killed by eating infected prey. If this book can help them in some small way it will have been more than justified.

David Hosking

March 1987

Hooded Vultures
sunning. Despite their
feeding habits —
gruesome in our eyes —
vultures take great care
of their plumage.
Sunning helps to enrich
the vitamin content of
preening oils,
conditioning the
feathers.

1

BIRDS OF PREY:
AN INTRODUCTION

Some vultures are among the world's largest flying birds. The Lappet-faced Vulture tops the African list for wingspan and wing area.

TOP INSET: Pygmy Falcons are amongst the smallest raptors, only the size of a large finch or a bunting. Despite their small size, they often tackle avian prey little smaller than themselves.

BOTTOM INSET: Few birds of prey hunt even in fading light, and none has specialised in noctural hunting as have owls like the Barn Owl. Despite some superficial similarities, owls are not thought to be related to the birds of prey.

Surprising as it may seem, providing a simple, clear-cut definition of 'a bird of prey' is not a straightforward task — but therein lies just one of the interesting aspects of this fascinating group of birds. With almost 300 different species falling under the heading of birds of prey, and leaving aside the 'invisible' features of the skeleton and other aspects of their internal anatomy that will aid university and museum specialists in determining their relationships, several readily recognisable common features would be expected. But not so: beyond a vague similarity in shape, the possession of a relatively large, sharply-hooked and powerful beak, suitable for tearing flesh, is the solitary obvious linking feature.

In any group of animals that is reasonably diverse, a range of diets and a range of techniques for exploiting those diets is to be expected. Thus amongst the mammals, there is the range of grazing vegetarians — in Africa, for example, represented by the many different species of antelope. On these antelopes prey the hunters, the flesh-eaters or carnivores, in Africa represented by species like the hyaenas and the lion. So it is with the birds, except that the wide range of seed and fruit-eating birds, together with those that eat small animals such as insects or worms, are in turn preyed upon by a much larger range of predators than is the case with the mammals. These predators are the owls, and the raptors, the birds of prey that feature in this book.

All birds of prey are flesh eaters, and the range of flesh eaten ranges from the humblest earthworm and beetle to quarries demanding extremes of power and hunting skills, such as deer and monkeys. By no means all birds of prey, though, are active predators: some are specialist carrion eaters (like the vultures) and indeed few will reject the opportunity to scavenge when it arises. The two groups of vultures are the obstacle to including powerful legs and feet, armed with sharply-clawed talons, as a standard raptor feature. Such hunting equipment is unnecessary in a

carrion-eater, and vulture feet (though perhaps recognisably allied to the talons of an eagle) are comparatively feeble, with short blunt-nailed toes.

Birds of prey range in size from falcons little larger than a small thrush or oriole to massive eagles and vultures. The condors of the Americas, with huge broad wings, are amongst the largest of flying birds with a wingspan often around the 3 metre (10 feet) mark. Like many groups of birds, the birds of prey have adapted and evolved over the ages to exploit the full range of their capabilities as flesh-eating hunters and scavengers. Several groupings are recognisable (for example hawks, vultures, falcons and eagles) and within each group adaptive radiation in size and habits is also to be found — there are big eagles and small, generalist and specialist feeders — all of which adds to their attraction and interest.

Though some birds of prey (like the Bat Falcon) hunt in the failing light of evening, the great majority are active only during daylight hours. Thus, though as would be expected their sight is extremely acute, they do not have the hugely specialised eyes and ears of those other flesh-eating hooked-beak hunters, the predominantly nocturnal owls. Most taxonomists view the owls as a close-knit group, which though similar in some of their anatomical features to the birds of prey (probably because beaks and talons have comparable functions to fulfill) are not at all closely related. Owls are thought to be close to the nightjars, while the birds of prey, strange as it may seem, may be related to the stabbing-beak flesh-eaters, the heron family.

When we talk about 'a species' it is worth outlining just what this means. Simply defined, a 'species' is a sort of bird (or any other creature) that will breed only with others of its kind, and not with other species. (Hybridisation — the mating of two different species — occurs quite commonly in captivity, for example amongst ducks, but is rare in the wild and normally results in infertile offspring.) Taxonomists (those scientists specialising in studying the relationships of living things) group similar species together in a *genus*, and similar genera in *families*. For example, the African Fish Eagle *Haliaeetus vocifer* is grouped with other fish eagles in the genus *Haliaeetus*, and *Haliaeetus* is grouped, along with other eagles (for example of the genus *Aquila*, which contains the Golden Eagle) and the hawks, buzzards and kites in the family *Accipitridae*. Sometimes features that are used to relate the various groups are outwardly obvious — there are readily recognisable features that link the falcons for example, or the sparrowhawks, but more often it is details of anatomical features apparent only to the museum specialist that predominate in the grouping of related birds, and these may not be apparent at all to the field birdwatcher. Equally, not all the features that the birdwatcher may consider

OPPOSITE: Museum specialists, following detailed anatomical studies, suggest that the birds of prey and the herons may share a common ancestry, the two lines parting many millions of years ago. This is a Louisiana Heron.

Black Vultures – the New World species – the wrinkled skin on their heads looking like a judge's wig, feed on Amazon freshwater dolphin carcases.

to be striking necessarily carry much weight with the taxonomist: some may be purely adaptive — for example to suit a feeding technique — hence the outward similarity of the Swift and the Swallow, which are unrelated except in their most remote ancestry.

A word on the 'scientific names'. These are used, and recognised, internationally. Each bird has two: the first, given a capital letter, is the genus, the second the species. Often this second name will refer to some characteristic of the particular species — for example *vocifer*, applied to the African Fish Eagle, is derived from the noisy or vociferous nature of the bird. Occasionally a third name may be added: this refers to a recognisable race or subspecies of the bird concerned.

One of the reasons for using scientific names is that vernacular or colloquial names can be misleading. One good example is the 'robin', a name which refers to totally different birds (except that they have more or less red breasts) in America, Europe and Australia. Amongst the birds of prey, by far the best examples of the confusion that can arise are to be found amongst the hawks and buzzards. Chapter 4 deals with this in some detail, but briefly 'hawks' to a European birdwatcher are long-tailed, round-winged woodland predators of dashing flight, while to an American they are the relatively ponderous, small, eagle-like birds of the open landscapes that Europeans call 'buzzards'!

As is the case in many other predatory species — lions or snakes for example — a

raptor's life is not a feverish continuum of hunting and killing. Most raptors are able, when times are hard, to endure several days without food. At the other end of the scale, when food is abundant, they may gorge to the full, sometimes to the extent that take-off is difficult! For most, a successfully accomplished hunting expedition will provide enough for their energy needs for some time, so often much of the day is spent at rest. 'At rest' includes time spent on preening, bathing, and other operations vital to the maintenance of good feather condition — perhaps of even more vital importance to the birds of prey because of their dependence on flight to hunt effectively. Flight makes heavy demands on energy supplies, too, so rest conserves energy. Often, raptors will wait until the heat of the sun has produced thermals — upcurrents of warm air — which provide additional lift without making demands on their intrinsic supplies of energy.

Thus, much of a raptor's 'average day' is spent at rest or in feather care, and relatively little on hunting. Feeding may occupy some time once the prey has been caught, and during the breeding season various additional demands on time become apparent. These include the often complex courtship flights, territorial protection display flights (to deter 'trespassers'), nest building, egg laying, and feeding and care of young. The last dominates the day of most female birds of prey during the nestling period, and involves both sexes in the training of the young once they have fledged.

The life-spans of birds of prey (as of other birds) are difficult to estimate with any accuracy because of the immensely high (to our eyes) infant mortality. Many eggs fail to hatch, many chicks perish before fledging, and many more soon after they leave the nest, when inexperience at hunting may lead quickly to starvation. Should they be among the 10 to 40 per cent of fledglings to survive into their second year, then for raptors the outlook becomes rather brighter. Many of the smaller species will live for 10 to 15 years,

the larger ones maybe up to 25 or 30. Captive birds, free of the hazards of hunting for a living, may live for twice these spans, but their longevity is misleading.

These, then, are the birds that have for so long captured our imaginations: birds of prey feature in ancient Egyptian wall paintings; the eagles have a long literary history as 'kings of birds'. The noble art of falconry is thousands of years old but the problems of conservation of birds of prey are very much a feature of the twentieth century. Add to this a wide diversity of form and function, and you have what must surely be one of the most fascinating and photogenic groups of birds.

Roman mosaics on the floor of the Convent of St Polyeucte in Jerusalem indicate the long association of the birds of prey with mankind.

OPPOSITE: 'Buzzard' to Europeans, 'Hawk' or 'Buteo' to Americans — an illustration of the problems of vernacular names in international ornithology.

Almost all birds of prey are masterly in the air in one way or another suited to their lifestyle, but it is falcons like the Lanner that create the greatest impression of flight skills.

2

BIRDS OF PREY
IN ACTION

The ability to fly — particularly the ability to fly as well and effectively as birds of prey do — makes a number of demands on the structure of the skeleton. Some of these adaptations are obvious and predictable — the 'conversion' of the arm and hand into a wing, for example. Others may be less so: to fly as adroitly as many raptors do, without expending too much energy in maintaining 'trim' (keeping on an even keel from side to side and fore and aft) the body must be as compact as possible, with most vital organs located close to the centre of gr vity. Many birds of prey, like the falcons, look compactly-built, but others seem less so, like the eagles or especially the Secretary Bird. However, a closer inspection of a Secretary Bird in flight reveals that it, too, is well-balanced. Weighty parts like the heart, flight muscles and digestive tract are still compact, and located close to the centre of gravity which lies between the wings — the obvious place for maximum flight efficiency. Those parts of the Secretary Bird which would seem likely to create problems in maintaining trim are its head and neck, and its legs and feet; however, not only are these roughly the same in the lengths to which they protrude (one forward, the other back) but they also weigh

Although one of the largest of raptors, the Andean Condor typifies the New World Vultures in its slender toes and short blunt claws.

much the same, and so are counterbalanced.

The major characteristic of bird bones is their combination of lightness with strength. This greatly reduces the energy input needed for flight. Most of the bigger bones are hollow, which retains both strength and rigidity, while reducing weight and allowing space for extensions of the air-sac system. Some major bones in vultures' wings are criss-crossed with bony fibres, which give added strength and are emulated by engineers in modern girder systems.

Though built on the same general lines as the skeleton of other backboned animals, there are significant advances, evolved for their way of life, in the skeleton of the bird of prey. Essentially, the raptor's skeleton consists of a strong central 'box girder' formed from the breastbone, keeled and strong to hold the large muscles that lower the wings on the power stroke and the less powerful ones which raise them; the short, rigid backbone (the vertebrae are fused together); and the strong flattened ribs joining the two. Within this, the vital organs are protected from the impact as predator strikes prey — a considerable impact in the case of a stooping falcon, for example.

Attached to this rigid box are the head and neck and the limbs. The components of the leg of a bird of prey are the same as in a mammal, even a human being, though the proportions differ greatly. The femur, or thigh, is short and stout, running almost horizontally forwards from the hip joint and usually out of sight in the body feathers. Thus the true knee is also concealed in the feathers, and what emerges, looking like a thigh, is in reality a shin (tibio-fibula); and the joint clearly to be seen in mid-leg, looking like a knee, only back to front, is actually the ankle. The section between the ankle and clearly recognisable toes is usually strong, and slender in many birds of prey, though robust in the eagles; on some birds it is covered in scales (differing little from those of the reptiles from which it was long ago derived), on others (as in the

A powerful beak is prominent in the Eurasian Black Vulture, but its feet are less strongly developed than those of the eagles.

Span, strength and length of claw typify the catching power of Golden Eagle talons.

aptly-named Rough-legged Buzzard and many eagles) it too is feathered. This is called the tarsus, and composed of the tarsus and metatarsus fused into a single bone.

Thus the raptor's leg, with its knee and ankle joints at some distance from the hip, and from the point of contact with the ground, and with these two joints (and the elastic ligaments round them) operating in opposite directions, serves as an extremely efficient shock absorber. It can take up the shock of landing, or striking prey, and also helps to 'catapult' the bird into the air on take-off, most useful if it is carrying heavy prey.

As a generalisation, the legs of most birds of prey are appreciably longer than they appear at first sight. At rest, or in normal flight, they are folded compactly, often largely within the shelter of the body feathering. However, when they are needed for use, whether it is to secure struggling prey in the air, on water or on the ground, it is essential that they are kept out of the way of the wings, which also play a vital role in prey capture – this is when their

unexpected length, evolved adaptively, solves the potential problem.

Although for many birds feet are for simple locomotion on the ground or for perching or for propulsion in water, the feet of most birds of prey are vital for them to

obtain food. Because of its powerfully hooked beak and ferocious appearance, it is tempting to assume that the beak is the major component of a raptor's weaponry. This is not the case: its main aids are its talons. It is the legs, with four powerful toes normally held in the shape of a cross to give maximum spread at impact, and each armed with a long, curved and sharply-pointed claw, that do the damage. The force of the impact between predator and prey forces the claws to close, and frequently a vital organ is penetrated in the process, killing or at least incapacitating the prey.

The beak, though seemingly so dangerous, is used to tear off chunks of flesh for consumption (this can be done with great dexterity by a female feeding her young with tiny morsels of flesh) though occasionally (especially in the falcons) it may be used to administer a killing bite, a *coup de grâce*, to the base of the skull.

The Marsh Harrier 'quarters' its reed-bed territory on stiffly held wings.

The massive beak of an Imperial Eagle — one of the true eagles.

Hunting techniques vary greatly among the birds of prey, and are in many ways related to their other limbs, the wings. In many raptors, the wings are long and broad, with the inner section of the wing (the secondary feathers, which are contoured like the aerofoil section of an aircraft wing to produce the *lift* necessary for flight) noticeably extended. This is the wing layout of birds best suited to long periods of energy-saving soaring flight, on thermals or updraughts at cliff-faces and hillsides, such as the vultures, which circle at great heights scanning the ground below for carrion or fresh kills; and the eagles, which from similar heights scan for signs of prey moving away from cover before attacking in a slanting glide, often taking advantage of the shelter offered by a rocky crag or the shoulder of a hill to gain the additional benefit of surprise.

Shorter, rounder-winged birds of prey (the hawks are typical examples) generally have longish tails which confer additional manoeuvrability. Their usual technique is to wait and watch in ambush, perched often inconspicuously within the canopy of a tree or bush. They rely on surprise, on speed in a quick dash, with high acceleration, and on a nimbleness through the vegetation which matches that of their fleeing prey, to secure a capture.

The harriers, birds of open terrain, be it meadow, marsh or moorland, are low-level hunters. Their wings, though long, are relatively slender, and the typical approach is to glide on rigidly-held wings low over the hunting terrain. Wingflaps are kept to a minimum, and prey is once again taken by surprise as it feeds amongst the vegetation. Lightning-fast reactions, a quick aerial turn (aided again by a long tail) and only a short plunge serve to secure prey. For those harriers hunting over wetland, there is an

TOP: Less impressive, the rather feeble beak of the Short-toed Eagle, thought to be primitive because its diet consists largely of snakes.

RIGHT: Lacking the double notch near the tip of its beak, the Goshawk typifies others of the hawk family.

Several birds of prey hover as part of their hunting technique, but only the Black-shouldered Kite does so with anything like the skill of the Kestrel.

Sharply hooked, the Osprey beak must tackle the slippery protective scales of its fish prey.

obvious additional danger that the plumage will get wet, or even waterlogged, in the process, so their exceptionally long legs are essential.

Other birds of prey actually specialise in catching fish, the Osprey and the African Fish Eagle being perhaps the best-known examples, though some other eagles, for example the Bald Eagle, also have fish as a major prey item. These do plunge into the water, the Osprey with an enormous splash. Though they rarely submerge deeply, or for long, they must quickly get airborne and shake the water from their plumage. The fish, often a large one, is carried head-foremost in the talons to reduce wing resistance in flight. Fish are particularly slippery prey, and the undersides of the toes of fish-eating birds of prey are strikingly rough and knobbly, like coarse emery paper, giving the best possible grip.

Probably the most familiar bird of prey to many people, world-wide, is the Kestrel, one of the falcons and a bird that has adapted well in exploiting the new environments made available by man in towns and beside major roads. Falcons typically hunt using sheer speed to obtain their prey: the Kestrel sometimes does but more often relies on its specialist ability to hover, scanning the ground below for likely prey. While hovering, it beats its wings and moves its tail to maintain station, and can do this in conditions ranging from a dead calm to a gale!

Even the 'typical' falcons vary considerably in their hunting strategies, though most are based on speed. Falcon wings are long and pointed: much of the length lies in the flight feathers, or primaries, the outer section of the wing that provides the propulsive force. In contrast to the vultures, the lift-producing inner portion is of normal proportions. Perhaps fastest of all in level flight is the Hobby. With long, powerful sickle-shaped wings, it looks like a giant Swift, and is even capable of outflying and catching Swifts in the air. Hobbies and the Red-footed Falcons of eastern Europe, also feed regularly on large insects like dragon-

The double-notch near the tip of this Saker Falcon beak, giving improved grip on the prey, is a feature of all falcons.

A male and two immature Red-footed Falcons. Insects feature largely in their diet.

flies. These again are caught in mid-air, but these two falcons show an unusual feeding habit of holding their catch in one foot and eating it while still in flight, like a child would an ice-cream cornet: yet another demonstration of the adaptive value of long legs.

Up on the moors and in the mountains, it is birds like the Peregrine and much smaller Merlin that hold sway. For their size, both are robustly built but very fast. Classically, the Peregrine will climb high into the sky, until almost lost to sight. Aloft it will wait, like a human fighter-plane pilot, circling and soaring until a suitable quarry bird flies past far beneath. Then begins the famous stoop: after a few powerful wing thrusts, the wings will be closed as the bird enters a power-dive that ends when it plummets,

full-tilt, talons outstretched, into its victim with an audible thud and knocking all life from its body. Should it miss an adroitly dodging prey, it needs must climb again to gain height for another stoop.

In contrast the smaller Merlin adopts a different but equally well-tried routine. Merlins patrol their territories at moderate flight speeds and at low level across the heather. Should they flush potential prey, usually small birds like pipits or larks, or encounter such a bird in flight, they accelerate to attack from behind, climbing slightly and attempting to achieve a kill after a brief high-speed chase.

The birds of prey are almost entirely daylight hunters. Few have specialised even in hunting in the low light levels of evening, as from then into the night, their

Most birds' eyes are large: even in the Starling, relatively speaking, the eyes are about fifteen times bigger than in man. The benefit of this larger size to the birds of prey is that it provides both larger and sharper images, vital for their often fast-moving predatory life styles. Though research into the powers of sight of birds of prey has concentrated on only a handful of species, it is apparent that birds of prey in general rate high on any scale of visual acuity, and that the Kestrel seems to stand out even in this company.

Kestrels sometimes hunt like other falcons, dashing out from concealment, scattering a flock of birds and snatching a victim in their talons during the ensuing panic – which in itself demands superb eyesight. But often they hunt from a hovering position, perhaps as much as 50 metres (160 feet) or more above the ground, scanning for tell-tale movements of prey on the ground below. Though this prey may be as large as mice and voles, often enough it is small beetles and worms that the Kestrel hunts from this astonishing height. The sheer physique for maintaining station while hovering[2] is matched by advanced anatomy, for the retina of the Kestrel's eye, the light sensitive area receiving the images produced by the eye lens, is almost twice as thick as in most animals. This naturally allows more microscopic light-receptive cells to be packed in, and at the fovea (the most sensitive area of the

role is effectively fulfilled by the owls[1]. Probably for the owls, their quite phenomenal powers of hearing are more important to successful hunting than their sight. Owl vision in poor light is exceptionally good, but their eye structure is adapted specifically for low light intensities rather than absolute visual acuity. For most birds of prey, though their hearing is good, amongst birds in general it does not rank as exceptional. Sight, though, is an altogether different proposition, as a moment's pause for thought on the hunting techniques of raptors as diverse as a vulture and a Kestrel will confirm.

[1]See *Eric Hosking's Owls*, published by Pelham Books.
[2]See Chapter 4.

Note the sharp claws but particularly the wide span of the talons of a Peregrine, both features assisting in the successful capture of prey.

retina) the Kestrel may have a visual acuity an astounding eight or ten times better than man.

Within the eye of a bird, suspended close over the retina near to the 'blind spot' where the optic nerve enters, is a little-understood organ called the pecten. In shape it resembles most of all a part-folded fan, and it is richly endowed with blood vessels. Current thinking is that the pecten helps supply oxygen and nutrients to the retina, thereby increasing its efficiency, and that it may help regulate pressure within the eyeball. Certainly, the size of the pecten is closely linked with the importance of vision in a bird's life: it is smallest in nocturnal birds, only a little larger in seed-eaters, larger in insectivores and largest of all, appropriately enough, in the keenest-eyed of all, the birds of prey.

The foods taken by birds of prey are varied in the extreme: almost any form of animal matter will be taken by one raptor or another, provided that it can be found or caught. Carrion features in many raptor diets besides the vultures, and it seems that small size is rarely an obstacle deterring the predator, many of the supposedly 'noble' birds happily feeding on ignoble items like carrion, or like beetles and worms. Almost always, it is animal matter that is the basis of the diet, though in the Palm-nut Vulture, even this general rule is broken, as its name suggests.

Size for size, the smaller birds of prey (in common with most other animals) eat rather more in proportion to their weight than do the larger ones. Thus a falconet weighing around 50 gm (1¾ oz) may eat three times its own weight of food a week, while the medium-sized Kestrel at about 225 gm (8 oz) eats about 275 gm (9¾ oz) weekly. Larger, the Common Buzzard at just under 1,000 gm (2¼ lb) eats less than its own weight weekly: about 600 gm (1¼ lb); and the massive Andean Condor, weighing over 10,000 gm (1½ st), eats only about 3,000 gm (6½ lb) weekly. Typically, the larger birds of prey are well able to withstand several days (at least) without food, a factor probably vital to their survival in the often barren and inhospitable terrain that many of them occupy.

For those birds that eat their prey whole, rather than feeding on carrion or dismembering larger prey, pellets provide a useful guide to their diet. Pellets, or castings, are composed of the indigestible remains (fur, feathers, bones, beetle elytra and so on, which can subsequently be identified) of the food eaten, collected in the gizzard and coughed up at regular intervals. Pellets are, though, only a guide, as they cannot reflect the proportion of the diet that does not leave such tangible remains.

Interestingly, in many of the birds of prey, the female is appreciably larger than the male. Often, it has been suggested, this will help reduce or avoid competition for food between the two sexes of the same species, a great benefit when times are hard or in habitats where prey is scarce and territories, in consequence, need to be large. The Sparrowhawk provides a useful example, the male taking mostly tit-sized birds, though capable of taking also the smaller thrushes, while the female starts at thrush size and can handle prey up to the size of pigeons. An element of cooperation may also be derived from the different prey sizes captured: again in the Sparrowhawk, when the young are in the nest, over the first few weeks the female guards them while the male hunts for all. But as his hunting capability becomes stretched to the limit as the young grow, the female begins to play the major hunting role, her power enabling her more easily to satisfy the demands of the young.

But this begs one question: why is it that the female is the larger, and not (as chauvinistic humans might expect) the male? The suggestion is here that the female is the natural guardian of the nest, eggs and young (at least in their early days) and thus derives benefit from her size. Also, in times of food scarcity, the male might be tempted to keep more food for himself, but her added size, and behavioural dominance at the nest, may ensure that he parts with his prey for the good of the brood.

Perhaps not surprisingly, there is much

OPPOSITE: Palm-nut Vultures have striking plumage, and unusual habits in that vegetable matter features in their diet.

less evidence of this sexual dimorphism in the more primitive raptors — for example, the sexes of predominantly snake-eating birds of prey (snake-eating being considered as a primitive feature) tend to be of similar size, as do carrion feeders like vultures and caracaras.

The predators are commonly considered to be amongst the fittest, in physique, of any given group of animals, a situation largely dictated by their way of life. Birds in general lead high-physique lives, because they are dependent on flight and the energy demands it makes, but amongst even them, the birds of prey are outstanding. Their highly-paced lives are powered by a heart and blood supply which though different from that of mammals, is at least as efficient. Pulse rates and body temperatures are in general appreciably higher than those of comparable mammals.

Most striking of all are the differences in the respiratory system and breathing. The lungs of a bird of prey are compact and highly efficient oxygen-exchange organs, but unlike the mammals, breathing is not an in-out function powered by a muscular diaphragm, with vital oxygen extracted only on breathing in. With a system of air-sacs throughout the body cavity (and sometimes extending into the larger bones), the birds of prey are able to keep a *continuous* supply of oxygen-rich air passing through the lungs. The motive force, or 'pump', for the air supply comes not from a diaphragm but from the rhythmic bellows-like action of the breast bone and ribs, changing shape and flexing under the forces generated by the powerful breast muscles as the bird beats its wings. Thus at rest, a certain amount of voluntary movement is necessary to supply the minimal oxygen requirements, but once the bird of prey is in flight, the faster it flies, or the more powerful its wingbeats (for example in a quick take-off), the more oxygen automatically enters the blood supply to the muscles and brain. This is obviously an extremely efficient system, and one well-suited to the high-powered lives that the birds of prey lead.

Raptors can produce some fearsome displays. The Crowned Hawk Eagle uses its 'crown' feathers to good effect.

Black Kites soaring over the majestic dome of the Taj Mahal.

3

BIRDS OF PREY
THE WORLD OVER

The Kestrel is one of few raptors to exploit oceanic islands to any degree: this is the Seychelles Kestrel, confined to those islands.

The Order Falconiformes is as cosmopolitan as any other order of birds and more cosmopolitan than many. Broadly speaking, this means that there are relatively few parts of the globe, short of those where the physical conditions (for example climate) make most forms of life impossible, where birds or prey will not be encountered. The exception to this generalisation is that, comparatively speaking, despite their remarkable powers of flight, the birds of prey have had little success in colonising the multitude of small and remote oceanic islands, where they are represented by only a handful of falcon species closely akin to the Kestrel, and each of these is very limited in its distribution.

Thus there are birds of prey in most habitats, from deserts to swamps, from coasts to the tops of many of the highest mountain ranges. The Andean Condor can be seen soaring close to the perfectly-shaped conical volcanic summit of Cotopaxi in South America, and the Himalayan Griffon Vulture can be seen from the shoulders of Mount Everest itself. Though in common with most other groups of animals, the greatest number of species of birds of prey occur in the tropics, other species penetrate to the coldest livable climatic extremes, for example the near-white Gyrfalcon, which hunts close to the Arctic Circle. There are no marine birds of prey, but several species (like the Osprey and the fish eagles) are closely adapted to a life in proximity to fresh water and largely dependent on fish for a food supply. In the forests and woodlands of the World birds of prey abound, and there are several marshland specialists and many that hunt in the tree-less tundra, steppes or plains.

Many genera of birds of prey, and thus even more species, are restricted to just part of a continent or zoogeographic region but others are more widespread. Thus the genera *Buteo*, *Circus*, *Falco* and *Haliaeetus* are widely distributed round the globe. So far as an individual species is concerned, the Peregrine is probably spread – even if very thinly – over more of the land surface of the World than any other bird of any sort.

As in many other avian groups, some of

A portrait of the
impressive white-phase
Gyrfalcon, well
camouflaged against the
often snow-covered
Arctic wastes where it
lives.

the birds of prey have developed seasonal migrations that allow them to exploit the summer richness of areas uninhabitable in winter. For example, many arctic or sub-arctic regions, the tundra in particular, are extremely productive of insect life in summer, and surprisingly productive in plant life. Thus they can support huge summer populations of insect-eating birds (mostly waders) and plant-eating small mammals like lemmings. Much the same is true at slightly more temperate latitudes,

and this summer benefit contrasts with the exceptional winter climatic severity of much of central and Asiatic Russia, Alaska and Canada. The climatic extremes encountered at higher altitudes also induce seasonal migrations. All of these areas share a winter climate that drives south the birds of prey that are able to survive with success in them during the summer.

Most such migrants head for tropical or near-tropical regions, where year-round the food supply is rich, and where, in

winter, local-breeding populations of birds are augmented by small-bird migrants from the north, which help feed resident and migrant birds of prey alike. Many such migratory journeys are long, often thousands of kilometres (or miles) in extent. Most birds of prey are not at their best as long-distance fliers, and seek wherever possible migratory aids, such as thermals, to assist in reducing the energy expended on the journey.

Many migrants follow traditional routes,

Even the seemingly most arid and evidently lifeless parts of the world support some small mammals and birds, and these have their predators among the birds of prey, especially falcons like the Lanner and Saker. This is part of the Judean desert.

INSET: Raptor-watching at Ras Nakeb Khumar in Israel. At such sites, raptor movements during spring and autumn migration may be massive, but a telescope is needed for certain identification of many of the passing birds.

Typical Peregrine Falcon habitat in northern Europe – and elsewhere in the world – open and remote from human interference.

often along lines of hills offering (by their upcurrents) some assistance to the migrants. Hawk Mountain, in the U.S.A., famed world-wide as a raptor observation post, lies on one such route.

A particular problem for soaring birds is posed by oversea crossings, as thermals are poor or non-existent over water. In consequence, the migrants opt for the shortest sea crossings, and as a result there are a number of places where raptor migrations, spectacular in numbers of both individuals and species, can be predictably enjoyed by birdwatchers, particularly in the autumn. These include Falsterbo, in Sweden, on the edge of the Baltic, where Scandinavian migrants are funnelled southwards into Europe. Gibraltar and the Bosphorus are at opposite ends of the Mediterranean, but both offer the shortest crossings from Europe into Africa. Eilat, on the coast of Israel, also offers one of the shortest sea crossings of the Red Sea, and lies further down the eastern migration route from Russia into the Rift Valley areas of eastern Africa. On days when weather conditions are favourable, tens of thousands of birds of prey may pass, spiralling upwards over warm hillsides to gain height before planing away south, losing height, making landfall at much lower altitudes before again spiralling upwards on thermals to continue their southward journey. On a good day, the sight of thousands of eagles, buzzards and hawks (normally rather few falcons) overhead is one almost without equal for the avid watcher of birds of prey.

The nesting-sites of the birds of prey are as varied as their habitats: it is usual for them to choose an isolated location and to position the nest in a fairly inaccessible position, but this is by no means inevitable. Tall trees and rocky crags in areas little

OPPOSITE: Jungles, such as this in Bangladesh, stretching unbroken to the river edge, are one of the world's threatened habitats as forestry and farming cut them away. Forest raptors are in consequence similarly threatened, especially those demanding large territories.

frequented by man are normal sites for many raptors, but the Kestrel is well known for its ability to penetrate urban, and even city areas and to co-exist there in close proximity with man. Even the Osprey, which over much of its range selects tall, often isolated, lake or river-side trees in which to build its massive nest, again distant from man, in several areas of North America nests on buildings amidst a hubub of mankind's comings and goings – in one case, nesting within a funfair!

Nests themselves vary greatly: many of the larger Accipiters, especially the eagles, build massive structures of branches, adding to them over the years until the nest may be in excess of one metre (3¼ feet) in diameter and over two metres (6½ feet) deep! At the other extreme, the falcons make no nest at all, either taking over the disused nest of another species, or laying into a simple scrape on a ledge. The site, though, will be just as impressive, with an equally imposing or commanding view of the neighbourhood.

As with carnivores and (frequently) relatively large birds, the demands of the breeding season, particularly the incubation period and the time taken for the chick or chicks to fledge, dictate the rule that birds of prey are single-brooded. Clutch sizes range from a single egg in the largest species to a maximum of half a dozen or so in some medium to small ones. Unfortunately, and to their detriment on occasion (see Chapter 5) many raptor eggs are attractively marked, usually with reddish spots, and over the years egg collectors have taken a heavy toll.

In temperate climates, larger birds of prey with long breeding seasons may begin breeding before the winter is anywhere near over, but most raptors in such climes have a breeding season matching that of most other birds of the area. This is highly functional in that it ensures that the young reach their most demanding period for food at a time when small birds (and also rodents and other prey) are at their most productive. Thus not only is prey available in peak quantity, but much of it is young

Adult and immature Bateleur Eagles bathing: parental care, giving vital experience in hunting (and here in feather care) may extend for several months after fledging.

and inexperienced, making hunting easier.

There are a few striking exceptions to this generalisation – for instance, the Eleanora's Falcon of the Mediterranean and North Africa. This, and a few other birds of prey, have evolved a late-summer breeding season, which allows them to capitalise on a different peak food supply – the rush of migrant small birds heading southward in early autumn. In tropical regions, 'winter', 'spring', 'summer' and 'autumn' do not dominate the climate as seasons, and are replaced by locally quite variable 'wet' and 'dry' alternations, or by a monsoon climate. Again, though, the demands of the raptor young for food coincide with peak productivity of local bird and mammal populations, and most small bird and mammal populations begin to reach this

stage towards the end of the rainy season and into the succeeding dry season.

Though in their early days the young are fed, with great delicacy of touch, by the female with morsels of flesh torn from prey brought to the nest by the male, they must soon learn to dismember prey for themselves. Thus from the time they are half-grown, the female leaves them more and more to cope with whole carcases. At this time, or soon after, they become much more active in the nest, moving about and often practising wing-flapping exercises. Once they fledge, the young (hardly surprisingly) lack much of the aerial skills of their parents. This they gradually gain, after many clumsy flights and crash landings. Obviously, for birds of prey that specialise in catching other birds (or equally elusive prey) there is no way that they can cope with looking after themselves immediately after fledging. In such species, the parents continue to feed the young (in the main) for several weeks while flight skills develop. 'Training sessions' are commonplace: the adult may induce the young to chase it, and not release the prey until after a considerable pursuit, or it may 'food drop', releasing the prey in mid-air for the pursuing youngster to catch. Gradually, the young gain in experience, and eventually become quite independent of their parents.

Food dropping, or food passing, is also the climax of the development of courtship display in the birds of prey, but there are several other stages. Simplest, perhaps, is the marking of the approximate boundaries of the territory by soaring flights high overhead. Any intruder (usually of any raptor species, not just the same species as the territory defender) is likely to be met with an aggressive threat flight, when the holder of the territory heads directly towards the intruder, flying fast and powerfully. Normally this is sufficient, but sometimes aerial sparring matches develop, often accompanied by the calls of the combatants.

Those raptors less adept at soaring – the falcons and many of the short-winged accipiters – have a more spectacular display. Climbing until almost lost to sight, they suddenly turn and plummet earthwards in a steep power dive, pulling out with a rush of air over the wings and shooting skywards again. There are many variants of this theme, including a descent in a series of swooping steps. Often again such displays are accompanied by penetrating cries.

Most thrilling of all are the joint displays when the sexes perform together: they may swoop and just miss each other, or indulge in aerobatic twists and turns around each other. Sometimes food passing may be involved, but more often the pair will lock their talons together, and with wings outstretched may tumble and cartwheel hundreds of metres towards the ground, before breaking apart and climbing away with powerful wingbeats.

The white head gives the Bald Eagle its name. Massive beak and noble appearance make it a fitting choice for the coat of arms of the USA.

4

FAMILY PORTRAITS

THE FAMILY *CATHARTIDAE* – NEW WORLD VULTURES

Although they are remarkably similar in appearance, with generally featherless heads and long broad wings with heavily 'fingered' tips, the New World or American Vultures are not closely related to their counterparts in the Old World, the African and Eurasian Vultures. The latter are grouped by taxonomists along with the eagles, kites, harriers and hawks in the huge, varied and cosmopolitan family Accipitridae. Not only do the New World Vultures look like their counterparts, they also behave like them, soaring effortlessly for long periods and relying on exceptionally keen eyesight to detect the carrion that forms the major part of their diet.

Though their beaks are large, strong and sharply hooked, unlike most other birds of prey their legs and toes are comparatively slender, with poor musculature and relatively ineffective, rather straight and blunt talons quite unsuited to killing. The arrangement of the toes, together with slit-like (rather than rounded) nostrils, the lack of a syrinx (or voice box) and other features are taken by some taxonomists as an indication that the origins, way back in fossil time, of the New World Vultures may be found in affinities with the stork and cormorant stocks of primitive birds.

The seven living New World Vultures are outnumbered by more than 20 species from the fossil record, stretching back at least 55 million years to the Eocene epoch. Some of the fossil remains are of really spectacular creatures: one, most appropriately called *Teratornis incredibilis*, had a wingspan of between 5 and 6 metres (16¼ and 19½ feet). Today, the family still boasts two of the World's largest flying birds in the California and Andean Condors, magnificent against the background of their remote mountainous habitats. Sadly the California Condor also qualifies for mention as one of the World's rarest birds, with only a handful of birds still flying free and not many more in captivity. The pros and cons of catching the few wild

remnants and using them in captive breeding programmes have caused conservationists in America to agonise for many years, and indeed the fate of the birds has been the subject of court cases.

At the other end of the scale, in both size and numbers, are the Black Vulture and the Turkey Vulture. Both are widely distributed in both North and South America, and the fossil records indicate that in the recent past, they were even commoner than today.

The New World Vultures are generally ground-nesters, the Condors choosing crags or often caves high in the mountains, while the smaller species breed in arid or scrub terrain, on the ground or on rocky outcrops, occasionally on ruined buildings. The Condors lay only a single egg, and normally do not breed every year, a feature which reduces still further the California Condor's chances of survival.

The Lesser Yellow-headed Vulture is the smallest of the three New World Turkey Vultures, and is confined to tropical America. This one was photographed in the Amazon jungle.

OPPOSITE: The blotched pink and grey skin of the Andean Condor seems repulsive, but note the spotlessly clean white ruff. Condors are amongst the largest of flying birds, and the California Condor is one of the rarest, with only a small handful surviving in the wild.

By an ironical twist of fate, this Turkey Vulture is scavenging off the carcase of a Red-shouldered Hawk – a road casualty.

The Black Vulture of the New World, feeding on freshwater dolphin carcases.

OPPOSITE: A portrait of the ornate head of a King Vulture, certainly the most colourful vulture and perhaps the most colourful head of any bird of prey.

THE FAMILY *SAGITTARIIDAE* – SECRETARY BIRD

So atypical in its structure and different in appearance from the other birds of prey is the Secretary Bird that it is placed in its own family with just one genus and indeed just the one species. The most immediately striking differences from other birds of prey are the extremely long legs and tail: seen soaring at a considerable height, the Secretary Bird can pose severe identification problems to birdwatchers because its silhouette is most unraptor-like and more akin to a stork or heron.

Although several other birds of prey have crests of one form or another, none resembles that of the Secretary Bird. At rest, the long plumes drape down the neck, but with the slightest breeze to ruffle its plumage, these feathers are raised into a strange halo, and it is their resemblance to the quill pens stuck behind the ears of old-fashioned clerks, or secretaries in days gone by, to which the origin of the name Secretary Bird is commonly attributed.

The Secretary Bird is unique among the birds of prey in that it always hunts on foot. It runs or strides on its long legs through the grassy areas of the African plains and scrub country – the bushveldt – that are its home. The prey it seeks is also terrestrial, ranging in size from large insects like locusts and grasshoppers, through lizards and small mammals to the eggs and young of ground-nesting birds.

Secretary Birds are best known, though, as killers and eaters of snakes, including venomous species. These they locate while they run quickly through the grass, often with wings flapping and often on an erratic course. Taking its prey by surprise, the Secretary Bird tries to get in a lethal kick, aiming just behind the head, before the snake strikes. Should a battle ensue, as often it does, the Secretary Bird wards off the snake with its wings, attempting to batter it into submission with wings and feet. Once the snake is subdued, if it is on the large side and still not dead, the Secretary Bird may fly up with it and drop it onto rocky ground to kill it, repeating the process if necessary.

Long legs partly concealed by the grasses of the African plains, the Secretary Bird stalks along in search of snakes. Note the 'quill pen' appearance of the head feathers, reminiscent of a secretary in days of old with his pen tucked behind his ear, and possibly the origin of the name.

Secretary Birds are thought to pair for life, and will spend most, if not all, of the year together. Unlike most raptors, the female is usually rather smaller than the male. Though they will not hunt close to one another, rarely are they out of sight of each other, and certainly not out of contact with their far-carrying trisyllabic wailing cries. Many pairs remain faithful to the same nest, built in a bush or flat-topped *Acacia* tree, year after year, adding to its structure each year until it becomes a massive edifice perhaps two metres (6½ feet) across. Both parents share the duties of incubating the eggs (usually two in number) and raising the young, which are fed – perhaps prudently – mainly on small mammals, rarely on snakes.

THE FAMILY *ACCIPITRIDAE*

With over 200 members, this is by far the largest family within the Order Falconiformes, the birds of prey. Not only that, but with representatives in every zoogeographical faunal region save Antarctica proper, it is the most widespread. Such are the number of species within the family, and such is the diversity in their form and function (though there are underlying common anatomical features that link them all within the one family) that they are best

considered in the groupings that are more or less readily recognisable by the birdwatcher in the field: the kites; the honey buzzards; the hawks; the harriers; the buzzards; the eagles; and the Old World Vultures.

Kites

If there is one single distinctive feature of this rather loose-knit group of birds of prey, it is that (even in a family renowned for its flight prowess) they are all exceptionally adept fliers. Most are relatively long and comparatively slender in the wing, and have long tails, while in some (like the Red Kite of Eurasia and Africa) the tail is both very long and also forked, probably enhancing flight manoeuvrability still further. In diet, most kites are generalists, taking relatively small, easy-to-kill prey like insects, slugs and snails, slow-moving amphibians and reptiles, and spending much time carrion-feeding, often communally. These features are often taken as representative of rather poorly developed raptorial ability, and as indicative that the

LEFT: Incongruous with such long legs and a long tail, the Secretary Bird perches awkwardly in a treetop.

A dark beak signifies that this Black Kite is of European origin.

INSET: Soft-plumaged, with its feathers delicately shaded by the setting African sun, the Black-shouldered Kite digests its meal.

BELOW: Familiar over much of the tropical and sub-tropical regions of the world, the Black Kite is usually a scavenger. The pale beak indicates that this is of the African race.

kites may be considered as among the primitive of the birds of prey.

Within this loose grouping are commonly included the bazas, or cuckoo-falcons, and the Bat Hawks (ranging from Africa, through south-east Asia to Australia). Cuckoo-falcons are probably largely insectivorous, and have a double notch in the upper mandible that must assist in holding such hard-surfaced prey. The Bat Hawk or Bat-eating Buzzard is one of the specialists of the group: it is probably the most nocturnal of all birds of prey, hunting (with exceptional speed in short bursts) bats, large insects and the occasional bird. The two Snail Kites, one from northern South America, the other (much rarer) from southern North America, are more obviously specialised for their major food item, fresh water snails, in having long, slender down-curved beaks ideal for extracting snails from their shells.

Most kites build twig nests — often untidy ones — in trees or shrubs, occasionally (like the Black Kite) using rocky ledges or even deserted buildings. Those, like the Snail Kites, whose habitat is extensive marsh-land terrain, more frequently nest just above ground or water level in dense reed beds. Clutch sizes normally range from two to four eggs, usually densely blotched reddish-brown on a pale ground.

More strikingly patterned, broader in the wing and shorter in the tail than most of its relatives, the Brahminy Kite glides over the plains in Pakistan.

At close range, the finely-streaked pale head of the Red Kite is a good distinguishing feature. In flight the long, deeply-forked tail (here just visible) provides certain identification.

The Black Kite, with its long tail flexing frequently, is amongst the most dextrous of the raptors in flight, and has been known to snatch a sausage from a picnicker's plate.

The Crested Honey Buzzard shares the long-tailed, small-headed appearance characteristic of the group.

Honey Buzzards

Despite the link in their common names between the honey buzzards and the buzzards (or hawks or 'buteos' in North America), specialist taxonomists link the honey buzzards more closely with the kites. Some would consider them to form one of three such subdivisions (the Perninae) at subfamily level. Honey buzzards are medium-sized, tree-nesting birds of prey, most of which inhabit various wood-lands and scrub ground through the Old World, and if their relationship with the kites is accepted, then probably also the Swallow-tailed and Hook-billed Kites from the New World should be grouped with them.

Typical of this group in many ways are the honey buzzards of the genera *Pernis* and *Henicopernis*, both of which feed extensively on the larvae of bees and wasps, which they dig out of nests or hives, often in soil or rotting timber, with both

A dense covering of small, closely-knit and tough feathers surrounds the beak and face of the Honey Buzzard, offering considerable protection from stings as it excavates wasp or bee nests.

OPPOSITE: Looking every inch a predator, a young Goshawk stands over its prey.

beaks and feet. In consequence, they must face the attacks of the enraged adults of these insects when obtaining their food: to protect them against stings, the honey buzzards have the front and sides of the head densely clad in a covering of small tough feathers — tough enough to prevent the stings penetrating. This gives a strangely small and rounded appearance to the head, which is distinctive compared with most other birds of prey. Otherwise, in shape the honey buzzards are broadly reminiscent of the true *Buteo* buzzards, although usually with a somewhat longer, narrower tail.

Hawks

Despite numbering about 50 species, the hawks are a comparatively uniform group of birds of prey. They are characterised by short, broad (sometimes almost rounded) wings and medium-long tails, and by their hunting techniques, which typically involve waiting, perched in concealment within a tree, for suitable prey to pass. This is captured after a short dash at high speed in pursuit. Most hawks are woodland or scrub

birds, and generally the prey they seek is small birds, though occasionally large insects, amphibians, reptiles and rodents are readily taken — for example by the Chanting Goshawks of Africa — if the opportunity arises. The broad and conspicuously fingered wings, coupled with a longish tail, give good acceleration (though not prolonged high speed) and above all extremely effective manoeuvrability, allowing the hawk to follow every twist and turn of its frantic, and seemingly much more agile small bird target as it darts through the trees.

One genus, *Accipiter*, alone contains around 40 species, which taxonomists consider as an indication that the group is comparatively advanced. Sizes range from the Sparrowhawk and Sharp-shinned Hawk with males perhaps less than 25 cm (10 in) in overall length, to the most robust and heaviest hunter, the Goshawk, where a large female may exceed 60 cm (23½ in) in length. Throughout the group, females are appreciably bigger than males, and they are often subtly, though distinctly, different in plumage.

Most hawks are tree nesters, building bulky twig nests (or adapting those of other birds) either in a branch crotch adjacent to the trunk, or in the canopy, but normally high above the ground. The eggs are typically pale in ground colour, but this is often almost obscured by dense brownish blotching. Clutch sizes range from three to six or seven eggs. The female is responsible for much or all of the incubation. The male supplies her with food during this period, and largely shoulders the hunting burden while the chicks are small and guarded almost continuously by the female. As they grow, and as their food demands increase, so her greater hunting capacity (based on greater size) is called into use. As an example of this increased capacity, while the male Sparrowhawk routinely takes tits and finches, and occasionally birds up to the size of thrushes, the female regularly hunts thrushes and may on occasion tackle prey up to the size of a Woodpigeon.

RIGHT: Africa is rich in birds, and in consequence is rich also in raptors specialising in preying on birds: witness the several species of both Goshawk and Sparrowhawk. The dove-sized Little Sparrowhawk often selects one of the many weaver birds as its prey.

FAR RIGHT: The African Goshawk – this is an immature – hunts over the bushveldt and in light forest. Though of medium size, it is heavily built, with relatively short and strong legs and toes.

LEFT: The Pale Chanting Goshawk predominates in eastern and southern Africa. It is separated from the Dark by its paler plumage and bold white rump.

BELOW: The Gabar Goshawk of African forests is one of the smaller Goshawks, smaller indeed than many European sparrowhawks. Some individuals may be almost black in plumage.

LEFT: Sombre in plumage, but with a distinctive barred tail pattern, the Cooper's Hawk comes from North America, ranging from Canada south to Mexico.

LEFT: The Dark Chanting Goshawk – a noisily vocal bird – ranges over much of Africa where reptiles caught on the ground often feature among its prey.

BELOW LEFT: Small is beautiful – an adult Shikra. These hawks range through southern Asia and Africa.

BELOW: An immature Shikra bathes in a small puddle left after an African rainstorm. Bathing removes obnoxious remains from the feathers and helps keep them in prime condition.

RIGHT: This Harrier Hawk has assumed a strange posture whilst bathing to ensure that all its feathers are wetted. The major identification features – a bold white band on the tail and the small yellow fleshy face patch – are clearly visible. Harrier Hawks' 'double-jointed' legs allow them to reach easily into holes and crevices in trees or the ground where prey may be hiding.

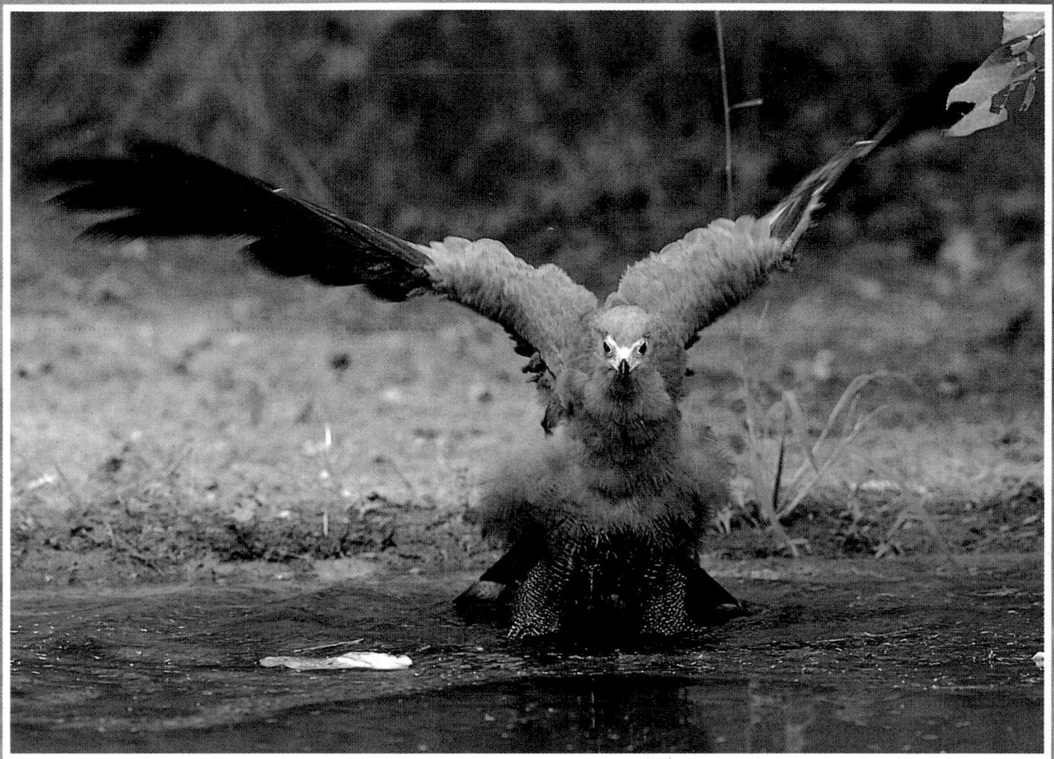

About to launch into flight, the Great (or Black) Sparrowhawk shows well the shortish broad wings characteristic of this group.

OPPOSITE: Alert, small and slim, the male Sparrowhawk waits for prey. Conspicuously long legs make the in-flight capture of its small bird prey all the easier.

The Sparrowhawk *Accipiter nisus*

Without question, the Sparrowhawk is the characteristic forest and woodland hawk across the whole of the Palaearctic region, embracing Europe, Russia and much of Asia. In North America, its place is taken by the very similar, but slightly smaller, Sharp-shinned Hawk *Accipiter striatus*. It is predominantly a bird of coniferous forests, but it will readily and successfully occupy deciduous areas where conifers are absent or in short supply. In many places, even open scrubland and farmland, with occasional trees or copses, serve perfectly adequately provided that they support a sufficiency of prey.

Until quite recently — perhaps the late 1940s and 1950s — Sparrowhawks were relatively common birds over much of their range. Then the population in intensively farmed areas of western Europe diminished alarmingly, and in many areas the Sparrowhawk became a rare bird. Blame for this decline was attributed to the post-war use of some organochlorine pesticides, which were characterised by an unexpected persistence in the environment and which tended to accumulate, particularly in predators. This caused unpredicted problems such as thinning of eggshells and behavioural disturbances which all contributed to an increasing rate of breeding failure. Only now, with most of the offending material no longer in use, is the Sparrowhawk population recovering to its former levels.

The bulging crop of the left-hand young Sparrowhawk indicates that feeding has been good.

In size, Sparrowhawks range from 28 to 38 cm (11 to 15 in), with wingspans from 54 to 67 cm (22 to 27 in), the females being appreciably larger than the males. The silhouette is typically hawk-like, with rounded wings and a longish tail, and the combination of a uniformly greyish (male) or brownish (female) back and a heavily barred breast (tinged chestnut in the male) helps avoid identification problems except with its larger relative, the Goshawk. The size ranges of large female Sparrowhawks and small male Goshawks overlap, so confusion is possible. Strangely, the Goshawk, though closely related, is one of the major predators on Sparrowhawks over much of Europe and Asia, taking both adults and nestlings.

In flight, too, the Sparrowhawk is typical of its family: normal flight is straight and often low, with short periods of wing-flapping interspersed with extended glides on outstretched wings. Particularly during the display season, Sparrowhawks may soar and circle high in the air, but when hunting their manoeuvrability can be seen at its best. It has been estimated that in short bursts, a hunting Sparrowhawk can accelerate to speeds between 60 and 80 k.p.h. (37 and 50 m.p.h.), but as much as anything it is the agility of the bird (aided by short wings and the long tail) that impresses. Every twist and turn of much smaller and seemingly more mobile target birds is followed with unerring skill.

Over the Palaearctic region, apart from a few small mammals and large insects (which are probably taken only in trivial quantity) the main prey of the Sparrowhawk is other woodland or scrubland birds. An amazing range of species is on record as prey, ranging in size from Wren and Blue Tit through to Jay and Woodpigeon. Such is the size difference between the sexes that

A fresh twig is added to the nest by the female Sparrowhawk. This bird is particularly heavily marked and lacks the usual eyestrip almost entirely.

most males concentrate on prey smaller than thrush-size, and most females on prey larger than thrushes. In itself, this helps avoid competition between the two sexes for food when it is in short supply during the late winter months.

Most Sparrowhawks seem to breed in their first year, though as is often the case, breeding success improves in subsequent years. Often the female will build a new nest each year, typically in the crotch of a branch close against the trunk ten metres (32 feet) or more above the ground. The nest is a ragged platform, with a shallow central cup lined with finer twigs, and in this the clutch of pale blue eggs, blotched with an infinite variety of chocolate spots and streaks, is laid. Clutches range from two to six or more eggs, with about four as the norm.

The female carries out nearly all of the incubation, leaving the nest only briefly.

During incubation, the male hunts for both of them, bringing food to the female on the nest. This continues after the young have hatched, as the female stays at or near the nest, on guard, until the young are well grown. During this period, she will have undergone a moult, replacing her feathers. This timing is not normal, but has a very practical merit: as the young grow, so the male (with his smaller hunting capability) finds them increasingly difficult to feed adequately. Thus, the arrival of the female to join him in hunting, with fresh and efficient 'new' wing feathers, comes at just the right time, and the sexes complete the rearing of the brood together.

Near the nest, the male will have several 'plucking posts'. Here he will remove the wings, tail, legs and beak of his prey with deft snips of his beak, and will pluck most of the body feathers – leaving a conspicuous and characteristic litter of feathers and

Harriers

The true harriers – within the genus *Circus* – are comparatively uniform in size and structure, and (usefully for the birdwatcher in the field) relatively easily recognised as harriers. That said, the separation of some species (particularly of females and immatures) may be appreciably more problematical, even at close range. Unusually among birds of prey, the plumages of the two sexes when adult are normally quite strikingly different, the male being predominantly coloured, the female often streaked buff or brown, perhaps as a reflection of her need for effective camouflage. The great majority of harriers nest on the ground, and the female does most if not all of the incubation, subsequently spending considerable time guarding the young. Typical clutches range up to six pale, often unmarked eggs.

Harriers typically have long, relatively slender wings, yet 'fingered' at the tips, and long slim tails. Their legs, too, are relatively long, and may be carried slightly dangling. Their standard hunting technique is to quarter their terrain low over the ground, with minimal wing flapping. When gliding for long periods, the wings are held stiffly, tips raised in a shallow V. The aim of this approach, as their habitat, for example moors, plains or reed beds, often lacks any sizeable vegetation, is to take the prey by surprise. Anything from large insects, through amphibians and reptiles to small mammals and birds (aquatic or terrestrial depending on habitat) may fall victim if unwary to the sudden drop of a hunting harrier. Exceptionally long legs serve, at the moment of capture, to keep the bird and its wings clear of the vegetation.

severed limbs around the plucking post. From the plucking post he will call the female to come and collect the food, or will take it to the nest, depending on the time in the breeding cycle. At all times he is cautious, as relations between the two seem often to be hostile, and males occasionally feature on the diet sheet of female Sparrowhawks!

By the time that they are about a month old, the young will have added short flights to nearby trees to their daily schedule of wing exercises. Now the parents will just drop prey onto the nest, or will carry it past, tempting the youngsters to pursue them, twisting and turning through the trees, before eventually the food is dropped and pounced on by one of the young. This form of 'training' of the young parallels that in other predators – for example lions – and must help prepare the young for the undoubtedly tough times that lie ahead until their hunting skills are fully developed.

OPPOSITE: The female Sparrowhawk, white eyestripe prominent, on guard at the nest. She will remain in close attendance, defending the nest vigorously against intruders, until the young are well grown.

ABOVE: With great delicacy of touch, she feeds the young with minute succulent strips of flesh torn from the prey.

A male Hen Harrier 'on guard' during the female's brief absence from the nest. Note the lack of a black wing-bar which is a feature of the otherwise similar male Montagu's Harrier.

Female Montagu's Harriers are distinguished from Hen Harriers by a much smaller white rump patch, here so small as to be hidden as the female shields her young from the sun.

Female Hen Harriers have a head feather pattern resembling the facial disc of owls. Young replete and falling asleep, the female stands guard.

On an unusual reed-bed
nest (usually the
province of the Marsh
Harrier) a female Hen
Harrier shields her
young from the fierce
heat of the sun. Note the
large white rump patch.

OPPOSITE: The female Marsh Harrier watches as her young scramble about clumsily on their platform nest amongst the bases of the reeds.

CENTRE LEFT: The male Marsh Harrier brings food to the nest.

LEFT: Harriers characteristically hunt on outstretched wings, held in a shallow V, 'quartering' their terrain low over the ground, as is this Hen Harrier.

Slimly-built and superbly silver-grey, the male Montagu's Harrier rests. The slender black bar on the wing distinguishes it from the otherwise similar male Hen Harrier.

Buzzards

If the true hawks, despite the number of species involved, form one of the most close-knit, structurally uniform groups of the birds of prey, then those members of the family Accipitridae grouped as 'buzzards' must be amongst the most heterogeneous. Granted around 90 species (depending on which taxonomic authority is followed) are involved in the subfamily Buteoninae, some measure of their diversity can be gained from the fact that they are gathered into almost 30 genera, only one of which has more than a small handful of species, and that is *Buteo* itself, with 26.

This is a cosmopolitan group, some members of which are almost 'everyday' in occurence. Its subfamily identity problems are not helped by a world-wide confusion over common names. The term 'hawk', widely used in Europe, with intended precision, to identify members of the genus *Accipiter*, is often applied by North American birdwatchers to the birds which their European counterparts would call 'buzzards'. Perhaps the alternative com-

Augur Buzzard: widespread and often numerous across the bush-studded plains of tropical Africa. The barred wing pattern is conspicuous as it perches atop a *Euphorbia candelabra* tree.

A Red-backed Buzzard —
typical of a *Buteo* in
silhouette, but offering
an example of how
misleading names can
be, as with its wings
closed, drab brown
feathers mask the russet
patches visible in flight.

Red-tailed Buzzard: here
the red tail of the name is
prominent in this large
woodland buzzard from
North America.

RIGHT: A Lizard Buzzard drinking, its distinctive throat patch just visible. Besides lizards, it hunts snakes and rodents.

A very dark Galapagos Hawk. All buzzards tend to be variable in plumage, even in a small population on such a remote group of islands as the Galapagos.

mon name in America, 'buteos', would be an effective compromise used world-wide to avoid mistakes, although this would itself generate some extra problems when not applied to actual members of the genus *Buteo*!

Some buzzards (or 'hawks' or 'buteos') are little bigger than a Sparrowhawk (for example, the Roadside Hawk of Mexico at 28 cm (11 in) overall length) while others cover the size range up to that of small eagles – for example, the White-tailed Buzzard of Central America which may reach 65 cm (25 in) from beak to tail-tip. Many buzzards are unusually vocal for birds of prey, none more so than the Common Buzzard with its far-carrying mewing cries.

With its young gorged to the full and fast asleep, the Common Buzzard remains alert. The remnants of its kill – a rabbit – await the next meal.

Well fed, a Common Buzzard stands at the carcase of its commonest prey, the rabbit.

OPPOSITE: The Rough-legged Buzzard breeds far to the north, almost as far as trees penetrate the Arctic. In winter, it migrates south in varying degrees depending on climate, food supply and population levels, occasionally appearing in considerable numbers at the extremes of its range.

The Grasshopper
Buzzard from tropical
Africa is relatively small,
and feeds largely on
insects.

INSET: In rear view, the subtle deep rust shoulder patches of the Harris's Hawk are just visible. Widespread over southern USA and through South America, this powerful hunter takes prey the size of rabbits and herons.

The pale Florida form of Red-shouldered Hawk, a bird of damp woodlands, eating frogs and fish as well as carrion and rodents.

OPPOSITE: A Red-shouldered Hawk: the delicate back markings show well in this normally-coloured bird.

Most build bulky nests in trees, or less commonly on rocky crags, with average clutches ranging from two to four heavily red-marked pale eggs.

The relationships of the smaller genera are far from easy to disentagle. Most are tropical, and many are forest birds, the majority emanating from tropical America. Some are specialist in their feeding: for example the Rufous Crab Hawk of coastal forests and mangrove swamps in South America, which as its name suggests hunts crabs, while the Black-collared Fishing Hawk, with its Osprey-like feet, catches fish in flooded marshland from Mexico south to Argentina. The Common Black Hawk and the Great Black Hawk, both of which occur from southern North American southward to northern or central South America, favour lakeside or riverine woodland or forest, and catch a variety of fish, amphibians and aquatic reptiles. The larger Great Black Hawk extends its dietary range to include small mammals and birds.

Such feeding diversity is more typical of 'buzzards' in general. Though never averse

With the source of its name clearly showing, a White-Eyed Buzzard from India rests between hunting expeditions. Frogs, lizards and insects are its main prey.

to carrion if it is available, they are capable hunters too, though they rarely tackle more difficult, fast-moving prey like birds. Perhaps they could be fairly described as the 'general purpose' birds of prey — and this fits also their appearance. 'Buzzard' wings are moderately long and broad, and usually 'fingered', while their tails are normally short to medium in length. They can often soar effectively for long periods (as does the Common Buzzard) and yet can, when needed, raise a surprising turn of speed and agility. Some are long-haul migrants, using their soaring ability to good effect to save energy whilst on passage. Despite the fact that most 'buzzards' are not particularly specialised, as a group they must be considered as very successful birds.

Eagles

The term 'eagle' is applied by the man in the street to the largest, and in appearance fiercest (and thus often called the noblest) of the birds of prey: indeed, regal is the appropriate term as eagles are popularly accorded the title of 'kings of birds'. In reality, though, the eagles are just about as diverse as the buzzards even though there are fewer species of eagles than buzzards.

In size, eagles range upwards from birds like the Short-toed (or Snake) Eagle, which are little bigger than many buzzards, through to genuinely majestic birds, almost (but not quite) rivalling in size the larger vultures and the condors. These include the sea eagles like the Bald Eagle of North America, and the more cosmopolitan

One of the smaller sea eagles, the White-bellied Sea Eagle is one of the most numerous and widespread birds of prey throughout Asia and Australasia. It frequents lakes, rivers and sea coasts.

LEFT: An immature Steppe Buzzard, often regarded as the northern race of the Common Buzzard.

Pallas' Sea Eagle – the
common fish eagle over
most Asian shallow
waters, often rich in fish.

White-tailed Sea Eagle: a
northern, primarily fish-
eating eagle, subject of a
fascinating
reintroduction exercise
in Scotland, where
Norwegian birds surplus
to requirements have
been released to replace
those made extinct by
persecution over a
century ago.

OPPOSITE: A White-bellied
Sea Eagle, perched and
to judge by its bulging
crop, digesting a meal.
When the dry season
starts to shrink the lakes,
it finds hunting fish
extremely easy.

Golden Eagle, which is one of the *Aquila* eagles. Both are about 80 cm (31 in) long. Larger is the Harpy Eagle, almost a metre in length with a wingspan up to and sometimes beyond two metres, from the jungles of Mexico south into Amazonia. This is a ferocious hunter, taking a range of jungle prey including active items like macaws and monkeys, but also slow-moving ones like the sloth. Arguably, the Harpy Eagle possesses as its hunting armament the most powerful set of talons of all the birds of prey: their largest claw matches in its

ABOVE LEFT: The African Hawk Eagle is known in Europe and Asia as Bonelli's Eagle. Eurasian birds are brown above and more heavily marked below, African birds are paler and greyer. This is a powerful hunter over rocky hillsides, taking rabbits, hares and small antelopes.

ABOVE: Splendidly boldly marked, the Blyth's Hawk Eagle sports a conspicuous cockatoo-like crest.

LEFT: The Hodgson's or Mountain Hawk Eagle is one of the largest hawk-eagles. Short wings and a long tail confer manoeuvrability on this essentially forest bird.

The majestic Imperial Eagle is a scarce bird, but the Spanish race, photographed here, is listed as a 'threatened species' largely because of past persecution and ongoing habitat destruction.

BELOW: The strikingly-coloured Bateleur Eagle adult seemingly lacks a tail. Though immatures have tails of normal length, the tail of the adult is extremely short and produces a characteristic silhouette, perched or in flight.

dimensions the largest claws on the hind foot of a grizzly bear!

Beneath the umbrella-term 'eagle' is grouped a wide range of genera, only a few of which contain as many as several different species. Taxonomically, the group is clearly diverse, and relationships within the eagles may well be quite distant. It is often said that the sea eagles, which form perhaps the best-knit large group (though only two genera and eight species strong, they have an almost world-wide distribution), show a detectable resemblance to the kites in both their anatomy and also in their general way of life, combining hunting, scavenging and piracy. Even some sea eagle displays are reminiscent of those of kites, from which group the sea eagles may well have been derived in the long-distant past.

The Crested or Changeable Hawk Eagle ranges from northern India into south-east Asia, and unusually, the largest birds come from the southern extremes of its range. It is very variable in plumage and the crest, common in Indian birds, may be lacking elsewhere.

FAR RIGHT: One of the world's most powerful birds of prey, the Monkey-eating Eagle lives up to the translation of its generic name *Pithecophaga*.

FAR LEFT: Huge numbers of Steppe Eagles breed across much of northern Russia and migrate south to winter in Africa and India. Enormous flocks may be seen over the Bosphorus, and other 'short sea crossings' on migration.

FAR LEFT: A Black-chested Buzzard Eagle, perched characteristically on an exposed tree offering a wide view of its hunting grounds on the African plains.

The female Verreaux's Eagle watches the male fly in with food for the well-grown eaglet.

Similarity in size
between the sexes is
thought to be a relatively
primitive feature, as too
is feeding largely on
snakes. The Short-toed
Eagle is also colloquially
called the 'Snake Eagle'.

The Harpy
Eagle from tropical
American forests
is another contender for
the 'most powerful eagle'
title. Now extremely rare in
the wild, it builds a massive
nest in the top of the tallest
tree in its huge forest territory.

Another group of eagles, loosely called snake-eagles or hawk-eagles, is considered to be relatively primitive and may also ultimately trace its ancestry back to the progenitors of the kites. Confined to the Old World, this group contains five genera, and many of the species involved (notably the Short-toed Eagle and the hawk-eagles of the genus *Spilornis*) have a diet which concentrates heavily on snakes. Many of the species have crests of one form or another, occasionally of the size and proportions more expected of a cockatoo. Only one, the Bateleur of the African plains, with its strange almost tailless flight silhouette, seems to take carrion with any regularity.

The harpy eagles constitute without doubt the most powerful group of birds of prey. Although only four species (in four genera) are involved, they span the globe in a strangely discontinuous distribution, with two American species and the two others in the Philippine Islands and New Guinea. All are huge, forest-dwelling birds with crested heads. Though broad, their wings are relatively short, giving them considerable lifting power: they may be able to rise from the forest floor or canopy, lifting prey the same weight as themselves — sometimes as much as 8 kg (16 16). Sadly, all are threatened by both the selective pressures exerted by collectors and hunters, and by the general destruction of their forest habitat. This produces a situation difficult to remedy, with the world demand for timber and the need for more hard currency of the emerging nations in which the harpy eagles dwell.

Largest of the sub-groups, and possibly amongst the most highly evolved birds of prey (certainly they are the most advanced eagles) are the 'booted eagles', called booted because the leg feathering extends down the tarsus, often as far as the base of the toes. Most authorities collect here eight genera, of which five contain only a single species, but this belies a comparatively uniform structure across the group. In general, these are large birds, with long, broad, heavily-fingered wings. All are superb in flight: many soar effortlessly, and several are long-haul migrants. The best-known genus is undoubtedly *Aquila*, which contains such species as the Golden, Tawny, Steppe, Spotted, Wedge-tailed and Verreaux's.

Most will take carrion when it is available (with the possible exception of Verreaux's) but most are also adept hunters, taking prey ranging from medium-sized game birds like grouse and francolins, through rabbits and hares up to young deer and antelopes. Often included in this group is the Black Eagle from Asia, which although

The Booted Eagle of southern Europe, north Africa and the Near East poses many problems to the birdwatcher in the field. It occurs in two strikingly different 'colour phases': a pale form, brown above and light below, and a dark, all-dark brown — various intermediates also occur.

An adult Bonelli's Eagle — photographed in Israel — feeds its nestlings on a typical crag nest site, inaccessible from below and protected from above by a massive overhang.

'booted' in having feathered tarsi, is much more frail in build than the *Aquila* eagles, and has commensurately feeble talons. It is extremely adroit in flight, taking (on the wing) eggs or nestlings from nest (sometimes even taking the nest as well). It also catches other slow-moving, relatively defenceless prey.

Eagles nest on ledges on precipitous crags or in tall trees, normally in country with a sparse human population. Many nests of the larger species in remote areas may have been in the location for decades if not centuries. The nests are large, sometimes huge after the addition of more and more branches and greenery over many years. Clutches are normally of a single egg in the largest species, with two or more rarely three in the others. The eggs, though variable, are typically rather rounded, whitish with sparse brownish or reddish markings. In some larger eagles, though both eggs in a two-egg clutch may hatch, quite commonly the older (and thus slightly larger) chick will kill its smaller, younger sibling.

Looking like a black Cockatoo, the Long-crested Hawk Eagle perches on an African *Acacia* tree.

A Crested Serpent Eagle sunning in a *Bombax* (or silk-cotton or kapok) tree. In flight, a noisy and frequently uttered scream and a bold bar on the underside of the wing ease identification.

The Tawny Eagle, resident year-round in the tropics, is often difficult to distinguish from migrant Steppe Eagles.

RIGHT: One of the largest African raptors, the Martial Eagle rests between hunting forays.

FAR RIGHT: The Lesser Spotted Eagle is a numerous bird in the vastness of its breeding grounds in Asiatic Russia. Here it is seen calling in its tropical winter quarters.

FAR RIGHT: Wahlberg's Eagle makes a speciality of dismantling the thorny nests of African Buffalo Weavers to eat the nestlings within.

The Golden Eagle waits, one eye cocked for the arrival of its mate. Surely this must be amongst the most noble of bird of prey profiles, and certainly one of the most powerful beaks.

OPPOSITE: Golden Eagle nests are often massive structures, some of which have been built up and refurbished annually by a succession of pairs, using the same crag or tree, sometimes for over a century.

Golden Eagle *Aquila chrysaetos*

With a distribution embracing much of the northern hemisphere apart from its polar and tropical extremes, the Golden Eagle must be regarded as amongst the more successful birds of prey. Most Golden Eagles establish enormous territories (often tens of square kilometres (or miles) in extent) in barren, harsh mountain country. Like some other predators, Golden Eagles have the ability to gorge while food is abundant, and to go without food for even several days when it is scarce. This allows them to endure and survive the prolonged spells of harsh weather, when snow and ice predominate, not uncommon during the winter months high in the mountains. Golden Eagles seem better at surviving in these circumstances than other ostensibly mountain birds like the Raven, Peregrine and buzzard – indeed only the specially-adapted Ptarmigan seems able to out-endure them.

Not surprisingly, living in such barren terrain induces a catholic taste in food: carrion is taken when available and live food is hard to come by; the range of live prey ranges from small rodents, through rabbits, hares and grouse, to young deer and birds the size of geese. Most prey is taken by surprise as the hunting eagle rounds the shoulder of a hill or sweeps out from behind a crag. The kill may be in the air or on the ground, but the large feet, armed with long, strong, sharp talons, quickly administer fatal wounds. Often fur or feathers are stripped from the prey before eating, and remaining indigestible material (bones, fur, feathers) is produced as large pellets or castings, coughed up and deposited beneath favoured roosting or feeding perches. As with other raptors, these pellets form a useful (but not infal-lible) guide to the diet. Large prey may be eaten in part on the spot, or sometimes dismembered. Arguments range over the peak lifting power of the Golden Eagle, but deer calves weighing of the order of 5 kg (11 lb) would seem to be about the accep-ted limit.

The name 'Golden' derives from the head and neck feathers, which are golden in colour in young adults, fading to straw-yellow in aged birds. The rest of the plum-age in adults is rich dark brown, appearing almost black in flight. Immatures can at once be recognised by the conspicuous white patches visible in the wing in flight, and by the white bases to the tail feathers. Like other large raptors, Golden Eagles make maximum use of air currents in flight to save energy. Take-off is usually downhill and into wind, after which the eagle uses slow, powerful wingbeats to gain some height before gliding away or beginning to spiral upwards, on rigidly-held wings, in a suitable upcurrent.

In flight, the length and breadth of the wings can be properly appreciated, but confusion can occur in distant view with buzzards. The Golden Eagle has an appreciably more prominent head and neck, a longer narrower tail (rarely if ever held in a fan while soaring) and a much more ponderous wingbeat. At about 90 cm (3 ft) long, and with a wingspan of around 180 cm (6 ft), the Golden Eagle is much

Clutches of two eggs are common, and often both chicks will hatch, but more often than not only one, the larger first-born Golden Eagle chick, will survive to fledging.

larger than the buzzard, but this distinction is not always obvious in distant view if no comparisons are available.

Amongst the few species of birds competing for nest sites in mountain terrain, the Golden Eagle seems to claim 'first choice', displacing Ravens, Peregrines and buzzards – though all of these become uneasy neighbours and frequently attack passing eagles. The eagles seem little concerned by the attacks until they are pressed home, when a Golden Eagle may flip over onto its back (with astonishing agility) to confront its tormentor with two fearsome sets of talons. Tall trees and inaccessible crags seem equally attractive as nest sites, and the nests built may assume gigantic proportions – almost 2 metres across and 3 metres deep (6½ × 9¾ feet) – as fresh branches are added year after year. In each huge territory, there may be several ances-

tral nest sites (sometimes the same sites will be used, by different pairs, for decades) which are used in an irregular rotation.

Both parents share the rigours of incubation – which may involve sitting out spring blizzards – for about six weeks. There are often two eggs, laid four days apart, and as incubation begins with the laying of the first, when the second eaglet hatches it is at a considerable size disadvantage to its sibling. Often the larger chick sets upon the smaller in the most brutal way, and often if food is in short supply, the weaker one will be killed. This is a form of natural selection, adjusting the brood size to the food supply: if food is abundant, the younger eaglet often survives, too.

Considering the massive size of her beak, the female Golden Eagle feeds the newly-hatched eaglets with the most delicate touch, tearing tiny strips of flesh from kills brought in by the male. Later, the female also hunts, and the pair bring part-plucked whole carcases to the nest for the eaglets to deal with. Fledging usually occurs about ten weeks after hatching, but the young will remain with their parents, gaining experience of the terrain and how to survive and hunt in it, for some months before leaving – or being driven out of – the parental territory.

The folklore of mountain people has many tales of baby-snatching by Golden Eagles, but these are indeed fairy tales. Lamb-killing, though, is not. On occasion, Golden Eagles will take lambs, but detailed studies have shown that these are almost always sickly or under-nourished – and indeed many of the supposed victims were dead before the eagles picked them up as carrion. Shepherds are alert to Golden Eagles as predators and may take brutal action in an attempt to remove them, which may go as far as setting fire to the nests. Gamekeepers, worried that eagles will disturb the very profitable business enterprises of grouse-shooting or deer-stalking, also take counter measures. Couple these to the threat posed by egg collectors and the insidious impact of agro-chemicals[1], and it seems remarkable that the Golden Eagle continues to hold its own.

Bald Eagle *Haliaeetus leucocephalus*

The Bald Eagle ranges across much of North America, favouring remote coasts and rivers and lakes in the wildest parts of the interior.

Named from its strikingly white head and neck, the imposing adult Bald Eagle is the national bird of the United States of America, featuring in heraldic poses on coins and coats of arms. It is the second or third largest of the World's eight sea eagles, with a wingspan reaching 2.5 metres (8¼ feet).

Huge size, white head and tail, and massive beak are the main features of the noble appearance of the adult Bald Eagle. All the sea eagles have strikingly large and particularly deep hooked beaks, even among eagles, and this huge beak allows them to handle their main prey, large fish, with reasonable ease. Handling fish is helped, too, by their huge golden feet, equipped with sharply pointed curved talons over 5 cm (2 in) long. Like other fish-eaters (for example the Osprey) the soles of the toes are particularly rough and knobbly, like the coarsest grade of emery paper, which helps them to grasp such slippery food.

Though fish, especially spawning salmon easily caught by Bald Eagles wading in the shallows of Alaskan rivers, form the main part of their diet at least for part of the year, at other times carrion (even domestic refuse on town rubbish tips) may be vitally important, especially during the winter. However 'noble' they are supposed to be, no sensible Bald Eagle will refuse the easy offerings of an animal carcase or the 'left-overs' after Brown Bears have been fishing and eaten their fill.

Bald Eagles breeding near huge colonies of seabirds will often develop a special expertise in catching seabirds, and some have been seen to catch and kill wild geese in flight. Sometimes, too, they catch fish by swooping low over the surface and snatching up a fish, or they may chase other birds of prey (especially the expert fish-catching Osprey) and force them to drop their catch, which the Bald Eagle then snatches and eats: a form of aerial piracy!

Bald Eagles set up territories in parts of the country where human beings are few and far between. In the more southern parts of America, the pair may remain within their territory (which is often several square kilometres in extent) for most of the year, but further north they have to migrate southwards as winter approaches and the water freezes. Even so, they only move as far as the first unfrozen water – often near rapids or dams – where prey is available. Once mated, the pair tends to stay together for life, or at least until one or other partner dies. They are very impressive birds as

[1]See Chapter 5.

A Bald Eagle soars on broad, 'splay-fingered' wings, against the dramatic cloud and mountain backcloth of Alaska, where summer conditions may approach in severity those of winters further south.

Almost invariably, Bald Eagle nests are in a prominent position, commanding a wide view of the surrounding countryside.

OPPOSITE: A group of Bald Eagles among the Chilkat Mountains of Alaska, wading into the chill waters to catch spent spawning salmon.

they patrol their territory, soaring on long broad wings with widely splayed feathers like fingers at the tip.

The female is noticeably larger than the male, about one metre (3¼ ft) long as against his 75 cm (2½ ft). This is most obvious when they sit close together on a prominent perch maintaining a watch on their territory, usually from a tree or rock crag giving a spectacularly wide view of the neighbourhood. The largest Bald Eagles come from northern Alaska and Canada, and at 6.5 kg (1 st) a large female weighs in at half as much again as her male. Male and female, though differing in size, are identical in plumage. Young birds have a mottled dark brown plumage all over, which gradually changes to the darker body, white head and tail of the adult over five years or more as a 'teenager'.

Before the breeding season starts, the pair will fly high into the sky, sometimes diving at each other in mock attacks. Once well aloft, they may spiral for a while and then suddenly fly close together and rear up, breast to breast, and grasp each others talons. Talons still interlocked, they will tumble earthwards in cartwheels, wings outstretched, often for hundreds of metres (or yards) before breaking apart and swooping away with the air roaring as it rushes over their straining wings, only then to soar up and repeat this spectacular diving display performance.

The huge nest is used year after year, with the pair adding still more substantial branches to it at the start of each season. It is robustly built to withstand the severe weather (blizzards occur even late in spring in the north) and the eggs and young eaglets are often cushioned and insulated from cold air by a soft nest lining of pine needles. Through the early part of the summer, the male will bring green branches to the incubating female, which she will lay round the rim of the nest. Always Bald Eagles build their nests in a prominent place, commanding a wide view so that the sitting bird gets early warning of approaching danger.

A normal Bald Eagle clutch is of two large dirty-white eggs, occasionally one, rarely three, which the female will incubate for about five weeks. Eggs may be laid as early

The immature Bald
Eagle shows all the size
and strength of its
parents, but lacks their
characteristic plumage,
which may take four or
five years to develop.

in the season as November or December in the south of the Bald Eagles' range in Florida, but perhaps not until mid-May in the sub-arctic areas of Canada when the thaw is late. The eaglets are in the nest for about ten or twelve weeks before they can fly free over the wilderness. In recent decades, nesting success has fallen, often sharply, from the old average of about one and a half chicks per nest, probably as a result of the effects of pesticide poisoning. This may cause eggs to be laid with thin, easily damaged shells so the parents often accidentally break them, or it may cause the adults to behave in unusual ways, resulting in infertile eggs and abandoned nests.

Once, Bald Eagles were common birds in North American skies. Around a century ago, persecution started. Hunters shot many for sport, and others were killed by man – amounting to thousands every year as a cash bounty was paid for each one killed – because they were supposed to eat too many salmon and kill too many lambs. Bald Eagles certainly eat salmon, usually after they have spawned and often when they are dead or dying anyway, and the same is true for lambs. Recent research has shown the old reports to be greatly exaggerated, and that the vast majority of attacks are on lambs (and fawns) that were dead or sickly already.

Sadly, in the last forty years, Bald Eagle numbers have fallen still more, and it is now a rare bird in most areas. Much of the blame for this must be directed at the accidental pollution of rivers with farming or forestry pesticides (often applied in a blanket over a huge area by aerial spraying). These sprays have contaminated the rivers, and in turn the fish and these have in turn poisoned the Bald Eagles, at the top of the 'food chain', that eat them. Even so, on certain favourite stretches of river in remote areas of Alaska and northern Canada, at some times of year gatherings of hundreds of these spectacular birds of prey still occur, and as pesticide usage is now much more carefully controlled, we can hope that they will once again become common.

African Fish Eagle *Haliaeetus vocifer*

The adult African Fish Eagle *Haliaeetus vocifer* is amongst the most easily recognised of birds of prey. Not only has it an extremely conspicuous white head, contrasting with the black and rich chestnut of the rest of its plumage, but it chooses prominent perches — frequently in dead trees by the water's edge. In addition, it often draws attention to its presence with a series of far-carrying, high-pitched yelping, almost laughing calls that most birdwatchers would consider to be one of the most characteristic, and evocative, of all African bird calls or songs.

African Fish Eagles may well be the most common and the most widespread of the larger African birds of prey. With a predominantly fish diet, they can be found beside almost all large rivers as well as many smaller streams. Many pairs are found along the coast especially where shallow lagoons provide easy fishing; no lake, freshwater or alkaline, is ornithologically complete without its quota of pairs, and this applies throughout most of Africa south of the Sahara.

Throughout the year, a pair of African Fish Eagles will keep close together, keeping in constant contact by a series of ringing calls. When one bird calls it is answered instantly by its mate in what amounts almost to a duet. When resting the pair perch side by side; when roosting at night, they usually huddle together on the same high branch.

Early in the breeding season (which varies considerably depending on the region and on the seasonal 'rains') calling reaches such a pitch as to be almost incessant. Frequently, the pair will take to the wing, soaring with wings held high, butterfly-like, in courtship display. Sometimes they will come together in mid-air, breast to breast, interlock their talons and tumble downwards in a series of somersaults, only breaking apart as they near the ground — and all of this against a vocal background.

As with so many other eagles, each pair may have two or three regularly used nest sites, one of which may be used for several years in succession, probably depending on the quality of the fishing nearby. Nest building is a continuing process: each year fresh branches are added, and if part of the nest collapses after a storm, more substantial repairs are made. Often the nest is large, certainly if it is long-established and some may reach 2 metres in diameter and 1 metre deep (6½ × 3¼ ft). Both sexes take part in the renovation, and each season a new lining of papyrus fronds or old weaver-bird nests is added before the eggs (usually two or three in the clutch) are laid.

Unlike the situation with many other eagles, the eaglets are relatively placid, and fights between siblings are uncommon. Even so breeding success (probably dictated by the vagaries of the climate, especially drought, and its influence on fish stocks) is variable, and often no youngster fledges. It is thought that many African Fish Eagles may live for around fifteen years in the wild, so the population level does not suffer from such occasional failures.

Even though by eagle standards the African Fish Eagle is comparatively small, it still has a wingspan approaching 2 metres (6½ feet) and may weigh between 2 and 3 kg (4¼ lb and 6½ lb). Its major dietary items are fish, sometimes taken as carrion, more often caught fresh. Occasional waterbirds and rodents provide variety in its food, especially if fish become scarce. As a hunter, the African Fish Eagle is a joy to watch. Compared with that other fish-eating specialist, the Osprey, it is swift and highly effective. Its usual target is a fish weighing about 500 gm (1 lb), swimming in the warm waters near the surface. From flight, or often from a watching perch an amazing distance away, the Eagle flies directly towards the fish, snatching it out of the water with one foot without discernibly interrupting its flight pattern at all. Larger fish (up to two 2 kg (4¼ lb) or more are on record) present more of an obstacle: the approach flight is slower, and the Eagle may sometimes partly submerge as it

In plunge, the immature African Fish Eagle here more resembles an Osprey than its parents, reinforcing the problems likely to be encountered with young raptors. There may be two, three or four graduated intermediate plumages such as this before the adult finery is obtained!

OPPOSITE: Within minutes of a kill, vultures patrolling at a great height begin to gather in large numbers over the carcase, each alerted by the sudden descent of its neighbour.

lunges, sometimes with both feet, sinking its powerful talons into the fish before struggling to become airborne again with its heavy load.

The feet are extremely powerful, the long, strong toes armed with formidably sharp, hooked talons. As an additional asset to help hold prey as muscular and slippery as fish, the soles of the toes are as rough as coarse sandpaper, with short horny spines to improve the grip. Once caught, the fish is taken off to a frequently used feeding perch and consumed.

African Fish Eagles are adept at piracy, robbing birds like Ospreys of their catch by tactics that in human terms could only be described as bullying. Even the giant Goliath Heron may be victimised in this way, and it is quite common for one Fish Eagle (often enough a hungry female confined by her incubation duties to the nest) to rob another.

Old World Vultures

Although the Old World vultures number only fourteen species, they are grouped into ten genera, which may give a misleading impression of diversity. In general appearance, they seem outwardly similar to the New World vultures, but there are some important differences (including the possession of effectively hooked talons) which indicate a different ancestral derivation, perhaps from eagle-like ancestors, for the Old World forms. That said, the naked, often wrinkled skin of the head and neck is universally recognised as the sign of the vulture, and this feature is common to most, but not all, of the Old World group. In general, their wings are long, straight and very broad (there are exceptions), and markedly 'fingered' at the tips: wingspans frequently fall between 2 and 3 metres (6½ and 9¾ feet), and with body lengths

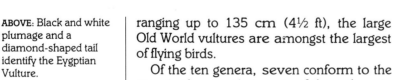

ABOVE: Black and white plumage and a diamond-shaped tail identify the Eygptian Vulture.

ABOVE RIGHT: Two White-headed Vultures bask in the sun.

RIGHT: The Palm-nut Vulture is unique among raptors in taking an appreciable quantity of vegetable matter in its diet.

ranging up to 135 cm (4½ ft), the large Old World vultures are amongst the largest of flying birds.

Of the ten genera, seven conform to the man in the street's image of the vulture in both form and function. This is indeed a close-knit group, all but three with a naked head and neck, with a basal ruff of feathers. Often the skin is luridly coloured, and frequently it is soiled with the most disgusting residues of meals.

Vultures soar for much of the time on broad wings held flat and straight, reliant on thermals rising from the hot, often arid land below or on updraughts created by cliffs, crags or hillsides. So dependent are most vultures on such thermals that they fly only through the heat of the day, when the heat of the sun has had time to warm the land. In consequence, vultures often go early to roost and are correspondingly late in rising the next day.

Exceptionally acute eyesight is essential for success: soaring vultures are widely separated in the sky, but once one of their number has located a carnivore kill, or carrion, and begun the descent to investigate, others rapidly plane down from lit-

erally miles around to join the gruesome feast. Though to human eyes sometimes viewed as sordid or repulsive, the unseemly scrum of vultures quickly disposes of a rotting carcase, and there is undoubted value in the task that vultures perform. Vulture behaviour perhaps appears more disgusting because the orgy normally involves much aggression, with tugs of war over favoured tit-bits accompanied by hisses and grunts.

The most striking anomaly among the vultures is provided by the Palm-nut Vulture, or to use its alternative name, the

Vulturine Fish Eagle, which eats several types of palm fruit as well as fish — the latter mainly as carrion. The alternative name may also give some clue to an ancestral link between the Old World vultures and the fish eagles. Similar in appearance to the Palm-nut Vulture is the small Egyptian Vulture, with a feathered head and neck and bare skin only on the face. It is relatively slender in the wing, as is the much larger Lammergeier, or Bearded Vulture, which also has the feathered head and long, diamond-shaped tail. At carcases, the Egyptian and similarly small-sized (60–65 cm; 23–26 in) Hooded Vulture lack the power to dispute the best food with their larger relatives, and must rely on speed and patience to snatch morsels where they can.

LEFT: Cape Vultures gather beside a carcase in South Africa.

BELOW LEFT: The Indian Black (or Pondicherri) Vulture dwarfs its smaller relative, the Egyptian Vulture.

BELOW: Like other vultures, the White-backed, with its scrawny neck and scruffy ruff, looks repulsive, but performs a vital cleansing task.

Ruppell's Griffon
Vultures rest among the
African thorn bushes and
digest their meal.

Hooded Vultures,
among the smaller
African species, with
relatively slender beaks,
gather round a dead
baboon.

Aerodynamically extremely efficient once the heat of the sun has created thermal upcurrents of air, the distinctive White-backed Vulture soars over arid land in Bangladesh.

FAR RIGHT: First on the scene, a Griffon Vulture adopts an aggressive posture in an attempt to deter new arrivals: the display is unlikely to be successful for long!

The Bearded Vulture, or Lammergeier, is a solitary bird except at the nest. Its feeding habits are unique, breaking open bones by dropping them in flight on to rocks, and then extracting the marrow.

Marabou Storks join
White-backed and
Ruppell's Griffon
Vultures in an unseemly
scrummage over the
residue of a topi carcase.

The Lappet-faced
Vulture, one of the
largest, is usually seen
only in ones and twos,
but normally is the
dominant species at a
carcase.

Griffon Vultures most
commonly nest on
crags, often colonially.

The Lammergeier, specialising in eating bone marrow, normally visits the remains after the others have finished.

Most vultures nest on rocky crags, and some also (or even frequently) in trees. Their nests are bulky and singularly repulsive. Clutch sizes range from a single egg, usually in the larger species, to two or three eggs, commoner in the smaller vultures, the eggs usually being white but soon becoming discoloured. Incubation periods range from 40 days in the smaller birds to 50–55 days in the largest, and the young may be in the nest for two to three months before fledging. The Griffon Vulture occasionally nests colonially on suitably rocky crags.

TOP: A group of medium-sized scavengers at the carcase of a sheep. The Black Kite on the carrion is flanked by Egyptian Vultures and a Raven.

RIGHT: An Old World Black Vulture stands guard at the nest. Clad only in short down, its scrawny youngster gives a clear indication of the reptilian ancestry of birds.

THE FAMILY *PANDIONIDAE* – OSPREY

The Osprey is placed in a family of its own, and there is only a single species. With the possible exception of the Peregrine, the Osprey has the distinction of being the most widespread of the birds of prey of the World. It actually breeds on all the great land masses – the Continents and the 'Island Continents' like Australia – except South America, where it occurs as a winter visitor, migrating south from North America; and except Antarctica, where the savage climate defeats even the Osprey's adaptive capability. It is interesting that the Osprey has also been able to colonise many small islands, a habitat only rarely exploited by other birds of prey, especially the larger ones.

Though buzzard-sized at 55 cm (22 in) long, Ospreys remind the birdwatcher more of a small eagle: the wings are long, spanning 135 cm (4½ ft) or more, fingered at the tips, but relatively narrow and carried in flight in a most distinctively angled way – like a capital M. Add to this the pale belly contrasting with a brown back, white undersides to the wings emphasising a dark blotch at the angle of each wrist, the equally distinctive head pattern, and a characteristic hunting technique and you have a raptor that is one of the easiest to identify.

A major part of the reason for placing the Osprey in its own family lies in the unusual structure of its feet. They are extremely well adapted to the capture and carrying of the Osprey's main prey, fish. Unlike the other birds of prey, the toes are roughly equal in length, and while they are normally held four-square in a +, the outer toe on each foot is so jointed that it can be held forward or back with equal ease, a feature found elsewhere in the owls. This helps greatly with holding and carrying large and very slippery quarry, as do the long, strong and sharply-pointed talons and the skin of the soles of the feet. The pads beneath the toes are covered in spine-like scales, which feel like coarse emery paper and ensure that a firm grip is maintained, even on the scales of a desperately wriggling fish.

The Osprey's diet is centred on fish, although not exclusively – carrion, small birds and rodents may from time to time be taken if the opportunity arises. It may well be the predominance of fish is the factor that has allowed it to colonise some smaller islands, for it is as much at home fishing in calm brackish waters or saline lagoons as it is in the freshwater lakes and rivers that European and North American birdwatchers consider to be its typical habitat.

Hunting Ospreys flap slowly over the water, normally from 10 to 50 metres (32 to 162 feet) above the surface, scanning for any tell-tale movement or shadow reveal-ing the whereabouts of a fish just below the surface. Sometimes the Osprey may pause, and hover clumsily, or it may glide on bent wings, but as soon as a fish is spotted, the Osprey pulls up into a brief hover before closing its wings and plung-ing, feet first, into the water in a cloud of spray. Rarely is the Osprey submerged for more than a moment or two, before emerging (often enough clutching a fish) and rising with some difficulty from the water. Once airborne, it pauses momen-tarily in flight to shake off surplus water, and perhaps to adjust its grip on its capture, before flying off to the nest or to its feeding perch. Once aloft, the fish is almost always held head-forwards, like a torpedo, to reduce wind resistance, and dangles well below the bird's body.

An average Osprey weighs rather less than two kilograms, and there are records of Ospreys catching fish of almost this weight, though 400–800 gm (14 oz– 1½ lb) would be a more normal size range. Round the World, Ospreys take an enormous variety of fish: perhaps the

Distinctive dark brown upper parts, near white below, with a brown-and-white slightly crested head are all plumage hallmarks of the Osprey.

In the USA, Ospreys are making a comeback after a serious pesticide-induced population decline. As here, they now readily build their bulky nests on man-made nest platforms.

major governing factor is that they take what is most readily available, but there is evidence that some individuals show preferences, and in other cases the presence of a well-stocked pond or lake (for example with carp, golden orfe or trout) close to a nest strongly (and not unnaturally) influences what the hunting Osprey catches! Even difficult prey like eels and flatfish are taken when in abundance.

In many areas, Ospreys are solitary nesters, but occasionally (as on the eastern seaboard of the United States) quite large colonies may build up. The nest is a substantial affair, used, and added to, year after year perhaps for decades. The nest

material is branches and twigs, with fresh greenery for ornamentation, and the chosen site usually a tall open-topped tree or a ledge on a cliff. In some circumstances (again most commonly in the United States) Ospreys abandon their traditional love of wild lake and forest country and nest on buildings (even in areas well-frequented by humans) or occasionally on the ground.

A normal clutch is three eggs, occasionally one more or less. The female does the bulk of the incubation, which lasts for five weeks, the male relieving her for short periods while she goes off fishing. Otherwise the male will supply some fish to the female while she is incubating, and once the young have hatched, it is he who catches and brings all food to the nest for the female to tear up and feed to the nestlings. This he does for about six weeks, after which the female also helps, leaving the chicks to devour fish that their parents drop onto the nest. After a couple of weeks, during which wing-flapping exercises seem to dominate activity at the nest, the youngsters fledge at 10–12 weeks old.

Osprey eggs are creamy-white, marked with reddish blotches, and rather sadly have been (and still are) regarded by egg-collectors as amongst the most beautiful, and thus desirable, of all eggs. In Britain, a combination of persecution by game-keepers and egg collectors drove the relic Scottish breeding Ospreys into extinction early this century. Breeding birds returned in the 1950s and they did so under the strictest protection. Despite constant vigilance and the use of sophisticated electronic protective devices, the Osprey still lost clutches of eggs. Fortunately, the recolonisation impulse was strong enough to withstand both egg collectors and the impact of agrochemical pollutants, and though still strictly under guard, the new Scottish population continues to flourish and expand. Most northerly-breeding Ospreys migrate to tropical areas to overwinter, and in doing so must run the additional gauntlet of hunters, particularly in the Mediterranean area, for Ospreys moving south out of Europe and Asia, heading for Africa. The toll taken by shooters is high — a substantial proportion of Scottish-bred young birds, all of which are marked with numbered rings, have been killed in this way.

ABOVE RIGHT: This historic photograph, taken by Cherry Kearton, one of the pioneer bird photographers, at Loch Arkaig in 1897, is probably the only one taken of an Osprey in the British Isles before the breeding population was exterminated, by egg collectors, early this century. Since the 1950s, under strict protection, Ospreys have returned to Scotland and increasing numbers now breed successfully.

RIGHT: The Osprey adopts an heraldic pose, braking hard with its wings as it comes in to land on the nest.

THE FAMILY FALCONIDAE –
FALCONS AND CARACARAS

If outward appearances alone were significant, so varied are the birds of prey
grouped by taxonomists in the family Accipitridae that it would seem a difficult task to
establish a separate family for the falcons
and caracaras, the Falconidae. This is
especially the case because although the
true falcons seem to form a natural, uniform grouping, the caracaras seem some
distance away. The similarities between the
Accipitridae and the Falconidae seem, on
the face of it, endless, starting with their
hunting abilities as carnivorous birds
equipped in general with hooked, tearing
beaks and with sharp talons. They lay
similarly rounded eggs, often handsomely
patterned in both families with rich reddish
blotches. Males are appreciably smaller
than females in both cases, and the
sequence of plumages from immature to
adult is much the same.

But there are differences, considered by
some taxonomists even to approach the
level that could suggest that the two families were unrelated. The 'obvious' similarities would thus be relegated to being
largely the products of 'convergent evol-
ution' – the development in different animal groups of similar 'tools of the trade'.
Most specialists agree that these differences at least merit family status for the
two, or even distinction at one level higher,
sub-order.

To the layman, some of these differences do not seem to be large ones. Many
of them are internal, but some can be seen
or watched: the falcon beak has an extra
notch near the tip, to give extra gripping

LEFT: Colourful and distinctive in plumage, the American Kestrel waits, on a typically exposed perch, for
prey to appear within range.
ABOVE RIGHT: Muscles tensed, wings ready for instant
take-off, this Red-necked Falcon epitomises the
hunter, right down to its wide-spaced talons.
RIGHT: Peregrine-like in appearance, the Laggar Falcon is favoured by some falconers for both its looks
and its flight prowess.

OPPOSITE: One of the
swiftest fliers, the long-
winged Hobby (here
tending young in a
typical conifer nest taken
over from another bird)
matches in silhouette the
Swift, one of the birds it
alone is fast enough to
catch.

Medium-small in the
falcon size-range, the
compact but powerful
Merlin nests on heather-
clad moorland.

power and to help in administering a killing bite to the back of the neck: a falcon characteristic not shared by the hawks and their allies. Unlike the hawks, falcons exhibit no real nest-building behaviour, simply laying their eggs onto a ledge or into the abandoned nest of another bird. The sequence in which the flight feathers are shed during moult also is different between the falcons and the hawks. In contrast, the often-quoted 'distinction' that falcons have long pointed wings and hawks short rounded ones is a generalisation difficult to back fully because of the variation in wing silhouettes across both groups. Last — and strangest — of these distinctions is the fact that adult hawks squirt their droppings away from the perch, while in falcons and caracaras they drop straight down beneath it!

Intriguingly, the falcons share some features with the owls (Strigiformes) rather than with other members of the Accipitriformes, namely: the lack of a nest-building instinct, the use of a bite to administer a

Heavily built but
beautifully proportioned,
every feather in place,
the Prairie Falcon waits
for prey.

RIGHT: Separated from its cousin the Kestrel by the lack of black spots on its chestnut mantle, the Lesser Kestrel also differs by feeding and breeding communally.

FAR RIGHT: The Striated Caracara, gawky and seemingly placid in temperament, seems a strange close relative to the falcons. It is a nimble runner.

RIGHT: Large-headed and long-legged, the Crested Caracara has a less ferocious-looking beak and feebler talons than the true falcons.

FAR RIGHT: Although one of the most diminutive of the falcons, only the size of a large thrush or small dove, the Red-thighed Falconet is one of the most attractively coloured birds of prey.

coup de grâce; the ability to hold a food item in one foot; the use by the young of hissing sounds and bobbing movements to show curiosity or alarm, or as a threat.

The smaller subfamily of the Falconidae is certainly the more diverse. Called the Herpetotherinae, it contains South American species and may represent an early offshoot from ancestral stock. Within the subfamily, *Herpetotheres* itself (the Laughing or Snake Falcon), which feeds largely on snakes, forms a link between the 'forest falcons' in the genus *Micrastur* (small fast-flying raptors, forest-dwelling and apart from a fluffy, soft-feathered appearance, superficially little different from the true falcons) and the caracaras. These have been disparagingly called almost chicken-like, and could hardly be more dissimilar from prime falcons such as the Peregrine or Gyr.

The caracaras — nine species in four genera — range south from southern U.S.A. to sub-Antarctic islands like the Falklands,

but have their greatest range of development in South America. Despite being categorised in four genera, they seem closely related: most are carrion feeders to a greater or lesser degree, and some have surprisingly blunt beaks and claws. They are long-legged, and walk about with speed and agility. Despite their feeble 'armament', they are aggressive and seem capable of dominating other carrion feeders at carcases and to be able to secure the best food items. Like the Common Buzzard of the Old World, they have learnt to associate roads with food, and patrol the roadsides in search of collision victims.

The second subfamily, the Falconinae, is itself subdivided into the falconets (or pygmy falcons) and the true falcons. The falconets are indeed pygmy falcons, the smallest being the Pygmy Falconet from the Philippines, which is only about 16 cm (6 in) long, the size of a medium finch. The other seven species (in three genera) seem closely related and are only slightly larger at

around thrush-size; they come from tropical or subtropical bush country in South America, Africa and south-east Asia. A typical hunting perch is a bush top, and a typical hunting foray is a flycatcher-like dart out from the perch to catch a passing insect, either on the wing or on the ground.

The true falcons, about 35 species in all, are remarkably homogeneous in anatomy and habit, and current taxonomic thinking usually places them all in the genus *Falco*. Of all the birds of prey, these long-winged, fast-flying sturdy hunters most capture the imagination. The nature of the prey taken depends on the size of the falcon, smaller species taking large insects and small birds, but most specialising in the capture of other birds, normally taken on the wing by sheer speed and surprise, often in completely open terrain. The stoop of the Peregrine — one of the larger falcons — is renowned and forms the basis for the Peregrine's centuries-old popularity as a favoured falconry bird.

Kestrel *Falco tinnunculus*

Without any doubt, the Kestrel is the best-known bird of prey for almost all Europeans: birdwatchers and the general public alike, in town or in country, are equally familiar with it. Not many birds can be identified by the majority of the populace, but the widespread distribution, commonality and distinctive hunting technique of hovering (earning the colloquial name 'wind-hover') put the Kestrel in this select band.

Falco tinnunculus, the 'European Kestrel', is a bird of the Old World, found over much of Europe, Asia, Arabia and Africa. To the north, it penetrates as far as the edge of the tundra, while in the tropics it stops only at the margins of extensive desert areas. Over much of this vast range

ABOVE LEFT: The Laughing Falcon is a strange, fluffy-plumaged aberrant falcon from South American jungles.

LEFT: As would be expected of a favoured falconry bird, the Lanner Falcon epitomises a combination of hunting power and noble appearance.

Kestrels are sedentary, but severe climate will force the most northerly breeders to retreat southwards in winter. Besides several subspecies elsewhere in the world (in Egypt, tropical Africa and on the Canary Islands), closely related species ensure that world-wide, Kestrel habits are understood. In south-east Asia, there is the Moluccan Kestrel *F. moluccensis*; in Australia *F. cenchroides*, the Australian Kestrel; and in North America there is the confusingly-named 'Sparrowhawk' *F. sparverius*, which is almost indistinguishable from *F. tinnunculus*.

At some 30–35 cm (12–14 in) long, with a wingspan of 60–68 cm (23–27 in), Kestrels fall in the medium-size range for falcons. Juveniles are pale brown, barred on the back and streaked on the front, and the adult female is similar, though a richer brown. The male has a grey head, brown-spotted chestnut back, and a grey tail ending in a single characteristic black band. All ages and sexes share the feature of black moustachial streaks extending downwards and backwards from the corners of the mouth.

In normal flight, a Kestrel shows a typical falcon build: longish tail, longish pointed wings, and a rather large head and neck. When hunting, it may use sheer speed, falcon-like, to surprise small birds or mammals, but most frequently it pauses to hover, often for long periods. Turning head

Brown head and barred back identify the female Kestrel as she perches on the rim of the hollow tree that conceals her nest.

to wind, it will maintain station, just as effectively though with less effort on a moderate breeze as in a complete calm, when more wingbeats are needed. Even in a gale, it will manage to hold steady by means of violent gyrations of wings and tail. Close inspection of the Kestrel head during this manoeuvre will show that the eyes – so acute of vision and vital in spotting prey – remain rock steady.

In this way, Kestrels will hunt prey ranging from worms and beetles, through small rodents to small birds. Often enough, hovering takes place at 30 metres (97 feet) or more above the ground, and to spot a small beetle at this range, and hold it in sight whilst plumetting down, talons outstretched, is tribute indeed to Kestrel eyesight. Kestrels are as catholic in their choice of habitat as they are in their diet. Mountains and hills, moorland and marshland, open woodland, scrub and farmland are all suitable, given prey and adequate perching and nesting sites. The good hunting ground of open motorway verges is now one of their most characteristic habitats. Even suburban gardens and city centres – the concrete canyons – somehow offer enough in the way of small birds and rodents to support Kestrels, which use high-rise building windowsills as substitute cliff ledges when it comes to the breeding season!

Kestrel display fights are far from the spectacular performances of some other falcons: usually the pair circle and spiral together, noisily, producing a most uncharacteristic-sounding musical trilling. In typical falcon fashion there is no nest: the eggs are simply deposited on a bare surface or in a shallow scrape. The nest site may be an open ledge on a cliff or rock face; a hollow in a rock face, or commonly in a large, normally little-frequented building like a church tower. Holes in banks or

ABOVE LEFT: Old, little-used buildings commonly provide nest sites for the Kestrel: here the female returns with food.

LEFT: Tree nests are less common as Kestrel sites, but always they are the disused nests of other birds, taken over by the Kestrels.

Hovering is the Kestrel's best-known hunting strategy, one that it has adapted well to the open spaces beside today's modern highways.

rolling over on their backs and striking out viciously with both sets of talons.

Kestrel fortunes have changed markedly over the last few decades. Once they were a common sight on gamekeepers' gibbets, along with weasels and stoats, Magpies and Jays. They did indeed take young pheasants, but now that these are reared in roofed pens, Kestrels are no threat. Many farmers have realised that Kestrels have a positive use, not just in helping to control, in a natural way, the numbers of harmful rodents, but also in acting as mobile bird scarers, disturbing feeding flocks of House Sparrows, or Bullfinches attacking fruit buds, and thus minimising damage far more effectively than a man-made bird scarer. In Holland, the newly-reclaimed polders were sown with various seeds, including the common reed, to stabilise the soil. Small rodents quickly rose in numbers to plague proportions on this rich food supply, undermining all the good that had been done. On the tree-less polders nest-boxes were erected to attract Kestrels, and rodent numbers were swiftly brought under control. Now, similar open-sided

trees also serve, as do the disused nests of other birds high in trees.

Kestrel clutch sizes range from three to six eggs, with a norm of four. They are rounded, basically whitish with a rich red-brown speckling that may often be so dense that the whole egg appears rufous. The female does much of the incubation, for about a month, and the young are in the nest for about seven weeks before fledging. As they get older, they defend themselves with aggression against potential predators,

The female about to depart on a hunting foray.

boxes, set on poles, are becoming an increasing feature of farmland where the farmer is combining rodent control with some thought for conservation.

Peregrine *Falco peregrinus*

Though never numerous, the Peregrine (or Peregrine Falcon) is one of the World's most widely distributed birds, breeding or overwintering on all Continents and major land masses except Antarctica. Over this enormous range, Peregrines differ appreciably in both size and plumage. As in other falcons, there is a considerable size difference between male and female (the larger), but also those Peregrines emanating from colder, usually northerly breeding grounds (in the sub-Arctic of Eurasia and North America) are appreciably larger than those from tropical or subtropical regions. There are colour variations, too, from almost black or dark slate-grey on the upperparts through to brown, and on the underparts (which are always heavily barred with blackish brown) ranging from almost white to deep gingery buff. All Peregrines, though, have a dark crown and distinctive white faces with conspicuous black cheek patches, or 'moustaches'.

It has been said that the reason for the Peregrine's cosmopolitan distribution is that it is a very successful bird, its success based on its mastery of the air. As a natural flying machine, the Peregrine is a masterpiece of evolutionary engineering, and can have few equals. These powers of flight are demonstrated not only while hunting, but also in the aerobatics of displays high over the nesting crags, where the pair will indulge in mock pursuit flights, plunging through the sky, or in the 'dog fights' between pairs of Peregrines and nearby nesting Ravens, themselves no dullards in the air. Such is the control in such skir-

mishes, and so long drawn out can they be, that it is difficult not to feel that besides territorial defence and the development by practice of flying skills, some element of enjoyment of the mastery of its element must enter into the Peregrine's role.

In level flight, the Peregrine is by no means the fastest of the birds of prey, though appearances may be deceptive. Its hunting prowess, and its popularity as a falconer's bird, derive from its spectacular oblique plunge after prey, called a stoop. From a waiting position circling high in the sky, it rockets down on unsuspecting prey with its wings almost closed. On a long power dive, the speed of a stooping Peregrine has been estimated at over 250 k.p.h.

Peregrines from different parts of the species' almost world-wide distribution may differ both in size (more northerly birds are larger) and in plumage colour. This very dark bird is of the South African race.

LEFT: With its true feathers beginning to emerge through its warm nestling covering of down, a young Kestrel stands on the edge of the nest prior to a session of wing-flapping exercises to develop its muscles.

(155 m.p.h.), but such speeds are notoriously difficult to measure with accuracy. That said, there can be no denying that the stoop, ending in the contact of talons with victim producing a thump audible for several hundred metres and normally killing the prey instantly, is one of the most spectacular sights in nature for those lucky enough to watch and appreciate the whole procedure.

Peregrines specialise in the capture of other birds, almost always taken in flight or after a pursuit-induced crash-landing. World-wide, several hundred prey species are on record and, in both Europe and North America the list exceeds 100. The smaller male will often take on small agile birds like waders (Dunlin for example) or even Swallows, while the more robust female uses her weight (often in excess of 1 kg – 2 lb 2 oz) to tackle prey as large as geese or Blackcock, sometimes lifting prey heavier than herself. Prey is often part-plucked before being eaten at a favoured perch.

Many Peregrines, by the nature of their coastal, mountain or moorland habitat, breed in areas remote from disturbance by man. Towering cliffs seem to be the most attractive sites, and particular ledges may be used for decades by a succession of breeding pairs. Occasionally, though, the habitat dictates otherwise: some Peregrines nest on hummocks in the tundra, or on the banks of rivers, and in the past many pairs bred in the disused tree nests of other large birds. In many parts, occasional pairs will nest successfully and often regularly on suitably tall buildings such as bridges, castles and city tower blocks, exploiting the urban feral pigeon population as a food supply.

LEFT: Peregrines take their prey by surprise, 'stooping' on it from a great height whilst it is in flight. Once they reach the ground, they begin to feed, starting with the fleshy breast muscles.

RIGHT: Viewed as a portrait, it becomes easy to see why, in times past, royalty were so impressed with the power and beauty of the Peregrine Falcon.

A single youngster is indicative of the problems faced by Peregrines during the 1940s, 1950s and 1960s, when contamination of their prey with some persistent pesticides reduced breeding success alarmingly.

Remote though their breeding grounds often are, early spring visits to appropriate habitat may reward the birdwatcher with the thrill of seeing the display – usually by the male, circling and diving and calling noisily before the cliff on which the female is perched. There is no nest as such: the eggs (usually three or four in the clutch) are laid in a scrape or simply on the rock. The sexes share incubation, though as the male does most of the hunting for food, the female takes the major time-share. The chicks hatch, tiny and fluffy-white, and are fed (with great delicacy) by the female on strips of flesh torn from prey brought to the nest by the male in the early days. Later, both sexes share the hunting, and by the time the young fledge (about six weeks later) the nest and its surroundings are the most appalling shamble of feathers, bones and rotting remnants of carcases.

The resilience of the Peregrine population has been amply demonstrated during this century[1]. During the Second World

[1]See Chapter 5.

Like other falcons,
Peregrines make no real
nest. They may adopt
the disused nests of
other birds like Ravens,
or simply lay their eggs
in a shallow scrape.

War, many Peregrines were shot in Europe because they were capturing homing pigeons carrying military messages. Gamekeepers and racing pigeon enthusiasts also took lethal toll. More sinister were the effects of the persistent organochlorine pesticides, which severely reduced breeding success in the post-war years. Today, Peregrine populations in western Europe are again on the increase, following the withdrawal of the offending pesticides and strict protection of breeding pairs by conservation bodies.

AUSTRALIAN BIRDS OF PREY

In stark contrast to other groups of animals in Australasia, many of the birds of prey (24 species in Australia alone) are found elsewhere in the world. The isolation and antiquity of the fauna of the Australian sub-continent is legendary: here one found the egg-laying primitive mammalian ancestors, the Monotremes, represented in the whole world solely by Australia's Duck-billed Platypus and Echidna, or Spiny Anteater. The majority of Australian warm-blooded animals, apart from true mammals introduced by man, are one step advanced on the Monotremes. These are the Marsupials, well known for their speedy gestation period and the delivery of tiny young, which, still almost in embryo form, wriggle into a pouch equipped with milk-producing glands, on the abdomen of their mother. Here they complete the major portion of their development: witness the bulging pouch of a Kangaroo carrying young. Marsupials are still present also in the Americas, but in much less variety than in Australasia.

ABOVE LEFT: A Black Falcon basks, wings spread to soak up the sun. Sunbathing is thought to improve feather condition — obviously of paramount importance to a bird of prey.

LEFT: Australia's largest raptor, the Wedge-tailed Eagle, is still widespread, despite the poisoning, trapping and shooting onslaught of bounty-hunting farmers attempting to limit its predation on lambs.

The bird of prey situation is very different: the Peregrine and the Osprey, for example, are almost worldwide in their distribution, and several other species are widely represented in Asia, like the White-bellied Sea Eagle. Of the twenty-four raptor species in Australia, only six are restricted to that country. Interestingly, all of these are amongst the rarest of the Australian birds of prey: whether this is due to the relatively greater adaptability and success of the incoming species, displacing the

ABOVE: Relatively broad in the wing, and rather buzzard-like in appearance, the New Zealand Harrier, an endemic species restricted to Australia's neighbour, New Zealand, alights beside carrion. Habits also show some resemblance to those of a buzzard.

RIGHT: Another species of restricted distribution, the New Zealand Falcon is confined to those islands. It is reminiscent in facial appearance of the Merlin.

perhaps more primitive or more specialised native birds, remains a matter for speculation.

The indigenous (or endemic) birds come from both major raptor families. The hawks and their allies are represented by the Square-tailed Kite, the Letter-winged Kite, the Black-breasted Buzzard and the Red Goshawk; while the falcons are represented by the Grey Falcon and the Black Falcon. In addition, the Australian Black-shouldered Kite *Elanus notatus* is confined to Australia, but differs only in minor plumage detail from the cosmopolitan Black-shouldered Kite, *Elanus caeruleus*, which occurs as close to Australia as New Guinea or Vanuatu. The Letter-winged Kite is often indistinguishable from it, except when in flight the undersides of the wing can be seen, revealing the black 'W' or 'M' that gives it its name.

Geologically and climatically, Australia is a land of striking contrasts, with the underlying physical features emphasised in a dramatic way by spectacular scenery offering widely varying habitats. In summary, a huge and largely arid interior, containing some of the most genuine of deserts as well as much dry scrubland subject to

The Australian Black-shouldered Kite is very similar in plumage to the Black-shouldered Kite of Africa and Asia.

occasional flooding at several-year intervals, is surrounded by a narrow, much more richly vegetated coastal belt. This contains varied habitats ranging from snow-capped mountains in the temperate south-east, through to the mangrove swamps and vestigial remains of rain forests along the tropical north coast.

Most of the kites are spread widely, if thinly, across the land mass, save for the Brahminy Kite which is strictly coastal and the allied Crested Hawk, which occupies the eastern coastal band and inhabits the edges of forest and bush. Of the hawks, both Grey and Red Goshawks are confined to the coastal belt, the former in the north and east, the latter in the north-east. Both are forest birds, the Red Goshawk favouring more open terrain. The pure white colour phase of the Grey Goshawk makes it one of the world's most striking birds of

To northern eyes, the Brown Falcon is reminiscent of a large female Kestrel.

Every inch as powerful and purposeful as its northern counterpart, the Brown or Australian Goshawk stands over some carrion.

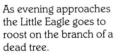

As evening approaches the Little Eagle goes to roost on the branch of a dead tree.

prey. The Brown Goshawk and the Collared Sparrowhawk are much more widely distributed through woodland and bush, especially along watercourses.

Of the three eagles, the diminutive Little Eagle is, although widely distributed, more or less confined to forest or woodland areas. The widespread Wedge-tailed Eagle is very much *the* eagle of Australia, though unpopular in the extreme with sheep farmers who consider it a major predator on lambs. Ancestrally — and no doubt even now — Wedge-tailed Eagles would have preyed on Wallabies and other marsupials, but enormous sheep flocks, the lambs often weakened by drought conditions, provided an obvious alternative food source. For years, Wedge-tailed Eagles carried a price on their heads, but the bounty hunters have failed to destroy the population. Soaring high in a brilliant blue sky, sheer size, wingspan and breadth of wing,

coupled with the characteristic long, wedge-shaped tail, make this a readily identifiable bird.

The remaining eagle, the White-bellied Sea Eagle, is smaller and confined to coastal areas, occasionally venturing inland along rivers or over seasonally flooded areas. This is predominantly a fish-eating bird, and the other fish-eating raptor of Australia, the Osprey, shares an almost identical distribution.

Both Australian harriers are more or less confined to Australasia as a zoogeographical region, and both favour marshes, meadows and arable farm land. The handsome Spotted Harrier, in adult plumage grey above and chestnut below, covered with the copious white spots of its name, is the more widespread of the two, the duller, browner Swamp Harrier being rather more confined to the coastal belt.

Of the falcons, many are widespread outside Australia, though as is usually the case worldwide, rarely is any species numerous. These are mobile birds (Peregrine, for example, means 'wanderer'), specialist hunters of other, smaller birds and unrestricted by habitat, so a wide distribution might be predicted. The endemic Black Falcon avoids the wetter areas, and is absent from many coastal regions as well as from much of south-west Australia. Also endemic, and also avoiding wetter areas, the smaller and paler Grey Falcon is missing from much of the extreme east of the country.

All the falcons favour open or light bush land, and the Nankeen Kestrel, very much the equivalent of the European/African Kestrel, is no exception, and is probably Australia's most numerous raptor. Certainly Australia's most diverse bird of prey, as far as plumage is concerned, is the Brown Falcon. Peregrine-sized but slimmer and more ponderous in flight, the Brown Falcon occurs in four colour phases — 'Dark', 'Brown', 'Red' (rather like a giant female Kestrel and predominantly inland) and 'Grey' (from the north-west). Immature plumages only add to this complex identification problem!

Dwarfed by the dead branch on which it is perched, the Australian Little Falcon (only thrush-sized) is a swift-flying hunter of large insects and small birds.

Equivalent in many ways to the Kestrel of Europe and Africa, the Nankeen Kestrel makes similar use of man-made perches!

Captive young White-tailed Sea Eagles, becoming acclimatised to the Scottish islands prior to their release as part of a recolonisation programme.

5

CONSERVATION

One measure of the pressures against raptors in the past – a gamekeeper's gibbet. Sadly, in some areas a 'shoot on sight' mentality still persists, despite evidence that it is ill-founded and unnecessary.

BELOW: Jaws clamped shut on a twig, rather than on the shattered legs of a bird of prey, the pole trap is one of the cruellest devices used in ill-considered attempts to protect game birds.

Over the past 2,000 years, birds of prey populations have seen widely changing fortunes. Over much of the time, they were held in what amounted to veneration, and protected by some of the strictest of man's laws. But then came gunpowder, the development of small arms – rifles and shotguns – and a shift in hunting practice. No longer did falconers and hawkers roam in search of quarry: instead, the various game animals and birds were gathered into intensively managed game preserves, within which they could be shot by sportsmen. Here the ultimate target was to achieve the biggest bag of game: keepers were employed not just to deter poachers, but also to ensure that the maximum number of target species was available to the wealthy owner of the preserve. So having for centuries been the backbone of the noblest form of hunting, falconry, the birds of prey found themselves, in a very short

space of time, right at the other end of the swing of the pendulum, regarded as harmful pests or vermin.

As vermin, they became legitimate targets for the gamekeepers to destroy. No longer were they specially protected, rather they had a price on their head, because a common way of paying the gamekeeper was so much per head of vermin destroyed. Hence the sad sight of gibbets, where the gamekeeper hung, for his master's inspection prior to payment, the vermin he had destroyed. On these gibbets, unfortunate falcons, hawks (and owls) joined mammals like squirrels, weasels, stoats and hedgehogs, and other birds of long-standing notoriety as egg and nestling predators, like Crows, Magpies and Jays.

The lands subject to game preservation by keepers ranged from mountainsides (deer stalking), moorland (grouse shoot-

Gamekeepers' mistaken approaches can be the same all over the world: shot Bonelli's Eagles in the Masan Valley, Pakistan.

much of the countryside in the so-called civilised parts of the world, like Europe, was in the hands of relatively few large landowners, or, as in North America, was considered to be available to anyone with a gun and an enthusiasm for hunting as a sportsman. In all these areas, the birds of prey were persecuted ruthlessly: they were trapped, shot or poisoned and their nests, with eggs or young, were sought out and destroyed.

They became also targets in themselves for hunters' guns, as a 'sport' rather than as vermin. In the early years of this century, some areas of the United States became famous for their hawk-shoots, generally where concentrations of raptors occurred on migration. One such was Hawk Mountain, in Pennsylvania, later to become famous as a migration observation post and a bird sanctuary. Today, sadly, such slaughter continues in a number of countries through which birds of prey migrate, particularly around the Mediterranean.

During, and perhaps even before, the 19th century, the collection, preservation and mounting of birds, (and other animals) by taxidermists became extremely fashionable, and not unnaturally, the birds of prey were amongst the most popular of subjects. Not only were sportsmen anxious to have their trophies mounted, but the taxidermists employed their own shooters and trappers to maintain the supply of corpses for mounting. This was an age of travel and discovery, and in consequence birds of prey from far-off lands also suffered at the hands of collectors as they had a special attraction as collectors' items.

This was the age, too, when egg collecting was a natural facet of the hobby (or obsession) of natural history. The eggs of most birds of prey were particularly prized, either because of their scarcity value, because of the challenge involved in collecting them by scaling tall trees or precipitous cliffs, or because of their sheer beauty. Though it must be remembered that, at the time, egg collecting was quite normal and socially acceptable, it remains difficult to justify in retrospect. Tens or even hundreds

During the 19th century, stuffed birds of prey were treasured ornaments, and raptor populations suffered at the hands of taxidermists.

ing), all types of farming land and woodland (pheasant and partridge shooting) to inland and coastal waters fresh or salt, where wildfowling was the sport. Thus there were few habitats indeed where the birds of prey were left in peace, particularly in the 19th and early 20th centuries, when

With a pencil to give an idea of size, these are the eggs of (top left) Osprey, (top right) Goshawk, (lower left) Peregrine and (lower right) Rough-legged Buzzard.

of thousands of clutches would have been taken, because as with stamp collecting, the really dedicated practitioner was anxious to have representatives of every colour variation in his collection, as well as of every species. Many raptor eggs are beautiful in their own right, even the most objective conservationist would admit, and their markings do tend to be variable, making them a particularly vulnerable target. Though it is easy to dismiss egg collecting as a thing of the past, and though in many countries the collection of eggs (especially of birds of prey) is forbidden by law, the hobby does persist as an 'underground movement' and is a blemish on many modern societies.

During this period, falconry as a sport had lapsed to being the pastime of only a handful of people in Britain, Europe and the U.S.A. Falconers found themselves as a lone militant group opposing the various forms of devastation that they saw afflicting bird of prey populations. It is ironic that once the critical state of raptors had been recognised, and appropriate legally-backed protective measures introduced into many countries, the falconers themselves were regarded as a threat by conservationists. True, the upsurge in popularity of falconry in the mid-twentieth century came at a time when raptor populations were at their lowest ebb and could ill afford the losses of birds like Peregrines taken into captivity for ultimate falconry use. In many places, this problem has been resolved by the use of licences, strictly controlled, to take birds of prey from the wild, by the prohibition of international trade in threatened species, and by the development by falconers of successful captive-breeding programmes, by means of which falconers' needs can be legitimately met by aviary-bred birds.

Over the last few hundred years, the population of mankind in many areas of the world has risen swiftly. Such an expansion in numbers places considerable demands on the natural environment, especially if it is accompanied by a rapidly progressing improvement in living standards and an increase in the trappings of civilisation, in which could be included items such as newspapers and magazines (demanding timber to make the paper) and foreign travel, opening up the wildernesses of the world. Without doubt, the major changes accompanying this progress have been in farming. To produce the crops necessary to feed the increasing numbers of mouths, over the last few centuries a great deal of natural environment — forest, scrub, moorland — has come under the plough, or at least into farming management (for example the drainage of grazing marshes).

This has obviously reduced the habitat available for many birds of prey: very few are as tolerant of mankind's advances, nor so able to exploit them opportunistically as the Kestrel has done. To the taking-in of land for farming must be added that effectively destroyed in the creation of towns and cities to house increasing populations: together, they amount to a huge area of the

Feeding young Tawny Eagles with meat. A plastic box replaces the nest, a paper towel allows renewable nest lining, and tweezers replace the parental beak.

RIGHT: Windows can kill, especially large plate-glass ones. A Sparrow-hawk dead after both it and its intended victim flew headlong into the glass.

temperate parts of the globe lost as raptor habitat. Nor is habitat loss confined to temperate climes with dense human populations: perhaps the most tragic losses are in the vast jungles and rain forests of the world. Here, emergent nations legitimately seeking to stabilise their economies and to raise living standards for their populations to the level of those enjoyed in the developed world, are harvesting with unprecedented speed (with the aid of modern technology and machinery) vast areas of centuries-old forest. So rapid and unnatural is the process of harvesting this valuable timber that it seems most likely that the forest will be lost for ever, with erosion and local farming ensuring that feeble secondary growth is all that will replace it.

But there are more insidious problems. In both temperate and tropical climates, agriculture has become increasingly dependent on artificial fertilisers, on herbicides and on pesticides in order to secure adequate crops. Excessive fertiliser usage, and water pollution with nitrates consequent on it, has a relatively distant and low-key impact on all except fish-eating birds of prey, though in the full context of environmental contamination it is extremely important. So, too, for herbicides. For pesticides, things are very different. Most pesticides are relatively unspeci-

This young Lammergeier has been temporarily removed from its nest to be ringed (or banded). Individually recognisable numbered rings allow the fate of marked birds to be followed, providing vital data in investigations of the ecology of scarce or threatened species.

fic in their action, though things are changing on this front. Thus they can be regarded as general biocides, killing most things that they contaminate in sufficient quantity. But most are short-lived in the environment, and are sufficiently well timed and placed to affect, normally, very little other than their insect pest target. Thus although their

Some poison is laid deliberately to kill birds of prey, a control measure now illegal in many parts of the world. This Sparrowhawk is more likely to be the victim of accidental poisoning, having eaten prey contaminated with insecticides.

derivation from wartime nerve-gases is terrifying, if properly controlled and used they should have little adverse environmental impact.

Sadly this has not always been the case. Man's knowledge often progresses as development and near-disaster succeed one another: so it was with the persistent organochlorine pesticides. These were developed largely during the war years, and were life-savers to vast numbers of troops who used them to maintain personal hygiene in the difficult conditions of war – particularly in the tropics. DDT is the best-known example, and after the war its cheapness and exceptional insecticidal properties were developed for peacetime use. Its role as a life-saver, to literally million upon million of mankind, was expanded when it was discovered to be the most effective way of dealing with the mosquitoes that transmitted the debilitating or lethal disease malaria in the tropics.

Used in combination with anti-malarial drugs, DDT virtually eliminated malaria as a health-threat to man.

Other chemicals, and other diseases were also involved, but for the clarity of the story, DDT shall continue as the focus of attention. In malaria control, one of the main values of DDT was its persistence: once sprayed on the wall of a room, it would continue effectively to kill mosquitoes for months. But this persistence brought with it unpredicted problems: in retrospect it is easy to be critical, but there were no scientific precedents for the researchers to follow, so 'blame' should be apportioned only with great caution. DDT persisted in the environment, generally being stored in the fat of contaminated animals and often in doses low enough to cause little harm. Once its insecticidal potential was appreciated, it was also applied to a wide variety of crops, and thus more and more animals, from worms upwards, became contaminated. Those birds that ate contaminated worms accumulated rather larger (though still rarely harmful) levels of DDT residues, but those birds of prey specialising in feeding on other small birds in quantity bore the brunt of the problem.

The position of the Peregrine, at the top of this 'food chain' of steadily accumulating residues, became precarious, as was the case for other predators. This was not immediately evident, nor was the problem identified for some years. The manifestation of impending danger started in the 1950s, when Peregrine numbers (and those of other raptors) began to decline. Ironically, a census of Peregrines was demanded by pigeon fanciers concerned that the *increasing* Peregrine numbers were threatening their favourite racing birds. The census showed dramatically otherwise: Peregrine numbers had slumped calamitously from pre-war levels to only a couple of hundred pairs, many of which were not breeding successfully. The cause of the problem was unravelled by some intricate scientific research by Dr Derek Ratcliffe. He measured the thickness of Peregrine eggshells in museum collections (where the date on which the egg was taken was on record) and was able to show that average eggshell thickness changed dramatically — the shells became much thinner and more fragile — at the time that DDT was introduced.

Examination of Peregrine eggs and dead adults showed lethally high levels of DDT residues in some, and worrying levels in others. Close observation showed that birds with sub-lethal DDT residue levels behaved abnormally, especially during the breeding season, and this, coupled with thin eggshells leading to greater rates of breakage, combined to reduce breeding success. Following this work, and work on fish and fish-eating grebes in the USA, mounting pressure from a number of conservation bodies, concerned that worldwide a catastrophe was approaching, led to the voluntary withdrawal of these materials in some countries, and their banning in others, except for strictly specified uses. But all this took time — several years at best, almost two decades at worst. During this period, though, much was discovered as to how such pesticides move through the environment, how they accumulate and in which creatures, and when they may become lethal. For example, DDT residues stored in fat may accumulate for months without causing harm, but if a period of cold weather causes those fat reserves to be metabolised to provide warmth and energy, then lethal quantities of the pesticide residue may be released into the blood. If the bird concerned is a migrant, death may take place hundreds of kilometres away from where the pesticide-contaminated food was eaten.

As time progressed, so ornithologists found more and more species, birds of prey and other carnivores (grebes and herons in particular) to be involved in these alarming population declines, and in almost all parts of the world. However, realisation of the potential magnitude of the problem dawned in time, and in most parts of the world it is fair to say that pesticide safety, testing and protective legislation have all benefited in a way and to a degree that would not have been possible without the near-disaster that befell the Peregrine and others. Though populations suffered at the time, it was ultimately towards a most worthwhile end. It is, too, a tribute to the birds of prey that though the environmental levels of these pesticide residues are still far from negligible (such is their persistence) population levels of most are recovering steadily. In the case of larger birds like the Peregrine and the Golden Eagle, this recovery is appreciably more rapid than was predicted.

To a large degree, this has been aided by strict protection laws, well enforced, and by the establishment of nature reserves or wildlife national parks providing habitat largely uninfluenced by man to form the basis of population recovery. Thus it is to the sufferings of birds of prey populations in the past that our current conservation-conscious society owes a great deal.

A falconer with a young Bonelli's or African Hawk Eagle.

6

FALCONRY

There is a great deal of uncertainty as to both where, and when, falconry originated. Its antiquity as a sport is undoubted, and most authorities consider that its origins were in the Far East (probably in China or nearby Mongolia) perhaps as early as 2000 B.C. Pictorial evidence of falconry in practice has been found from ruins in the Near East, in what was once Assyria, where a carving of a falconer and his hawk dating from around 750 B.C., in the reign of King Sargon, has been uncovered by archaeologists. Of written accounts, the earliest authentic record is in a Japanese text dated at 244 A.D.

Falconry was at its peak from the fifth to the fifteenth century A.D. It has been suggested that keeping and training falcons was an art of some sophistication, more in tune with settled noble families, whether in the East or in Europe. Hawking, in contrast, would suit well the nomadic herdsmen of mediaeval times, and it seems probable that the sport spread to Europe with the succeeding waves of warlike horsemen that swept across Asia and, under Attila the Hun, made successful invasions into Europe.

There is much pictorial and written evidence of the popularity of falconry at this time both in Christian Europe and in the Islamic countries of the Middle East. Among the most spectacular illustrations is that in the Bayeux Tapestry, woven after the Norman Conquest of England in 1066, where it is thought that by showing soldiers carrying hawks on the wrist, a long-term desire for peace was implied as the hawks were a symbol indicative of times allowing peaceable recreation activities.

Falconry was governed by meticulously observed social codes, backed by laws meting out savage punishments to those who transgressed, or even worse, persecuted or harmed birds of prey, or their nests, in the wild: an element of protective conservation far in advance of its time.

A fifteenth century publication, the *Boke of Saint Albans*, categorises the social classes and identifies their appropriate bird of prey — sometimes even specifying its sex. For the 'poor man', the appropriate hawk was a male Goshawk; for the yeoman, the female Goshawk. The priest had the female Sparrowhawk, his clerk the male, or 'musket'. Immediately a major divide is apparent: the lower orders of society used hawks, while the nobility used falcons. Ascending the social ladder, the Hobby (smallest of the commoner falcons) went to the page; the Merlin to the Lady. The Saker went to the knight, the Lanner to his squire. The real nobles started with the Baron, who was accorded the male (tiercel) Peregrine; the other forms of Peregrine went to the Dukes and Earls, while the so-called 'falcon gentle' — the female Peregrine — belonged to the Prince. To the King went the Gyrfalcon (and its male, called 'jerkin') while, top of the court social ladder, the Emperor enjoyed the power, weight and hunting prowess of the Golden Eagle.

Today, a falconer may own and train whichever bird he wishes, but there still remains the feeling that the falcons are the cream, the noblest of the birds of prey, while the hawks — short-wings — are more workaday birds. In fact, however, each group is so skilful and dashing when hunting in its own environment that such distinctions have little real meaning.

In the past, all well-furbished establishments from the manor house upwards had their 'mews' — a sheltered area, screened from disturbance, where the birds of prey were kept tethered, some to outside blocks, others to perches under shelter. In charge of the mews was the senior falconer, a man of some importance. Birds of prey had considerable value and often featured in ransom payments. Even today, the possession of a bird of prey constitutes a status symbol in lands as far apart as the U.S.A., Britain, Germany and Saudi Arabia.

This modern re-affirmation of the pride-of-place accorded to birds of prey has also been to their detriment, leading to egg collecting, and the stealing of nestlings, etc.

Much of the mediaeval terminology and classification of birds of prey persists in modern falconry. Thus falconers normally call the hawks 'short-wings' and the falcons

To the outsider, the most obvious links with this elaborate past are the trappings of falconry: the equipment that falconers use, which has indeed changed little over the centuries. Most conspicuous are the hoods, placed over the birds' heads whilst they are on the wrist and not hunting. The purpose of the hood is simple: it prevents sudden movements, passing birds and so on, from disturbing the falcon or tempting it to set off in pursuit of the wrong quarry. Most hoods are made in soft leather, usually of at least two colours, and are set off with leather ties and, often, with a small plume of

LEFT: The young Peregrine Falcon wears an elaborate and elegantly made soft leather hood to keep it calm whilst travelling.

'long-wings'; other distinctive terms include 'sakret' (Saker), 'lanneret' (Lanner) and 'jack-merlin' (Merlin) — all obvious diminutives. The term 'falcon' is, strictly speaking, applied solely to the female Peregrine. The male Peregrine is called a tiercel, from the Latin *tertius*, a third, because it is roughly one-third smaller than the female, as in many raptor species. Today, as in the past, the greater hunting power of the female is often preferred by the falconer.

Until the 1970s, falconers obtained their birds from the wild, captive breeding being almost unknown. This has given rise to an additional component of the falconry vocabulary: birds taken from the nest were called 'eyasses', while those trapped flying free were called 'passagers' if in first-year plumage, or 'haggards' if adult. Moult (when old worn feathers are shed and replaced) in the larger birds of prey especially may be an erratic and long-drawn-out process, but for most falcons and hawks it is an annual, usually autumn, event; once a captive bird of prey has moulted in the mews, it is said to be 'intermewed'. More recently, captive breeding has to a degree replaced the removal of birds from wild populations threatened by many adverse factors[1], and in many countries a licence is now necessary to take into captivity for falconry any wild bird of prey.

Falconers are now at the forefront of avian captive-breeding techniques. Here Peregrine eggs are inspected in an incubator. The young, conceived by artificial insemination, may be used for falconry or returned to the wild.

[1]See Chapter 5.

ornamental feathers on the crown. Second, and at least as important, are the leather thongs (or 'jesses') looped round the bird's legs. These the falconer grasps in his gloved fist to prevent escape or premature flight and to help the falcon maintain its balance. Jesses tend to stream out behind the flying bird when it is let slip to hunt, and are one way the birdwatcher has of distinguishing an escaped falconry bird of prey from what would otherwise be a sighting of a rare, or even exceptionally rare, genuinely wild bird. While at rest on its block or perch, the jesses are looped onto a leather 'thong', which with its swivel joints closely resembles a dog's leash, attached to the base of the perch.

Classically, falconers would have attached small bells to the legs above the jesses, again with a soft leather thong. This is to aid in locating the falcon once it has come to the ground with its prey. Though many falconers still use this technique, others increasingly take advantage of modern technology, and fit miniaturised radio transmitters to find lost birds. Although there are other specialised items of equipment (for example, for 'imping', the process of replacing a broken wing or tail feather, vital for effective flight, by inserting part of the shaft and vane of a spare feather as a sort of graft into the stump of the old feather), the remaining universal piece of equipment is the lure. Simply described, this is little more than a mock meal (for example a chunk of rabbit fur) attached to a long cord. Whirled around, this serves to tempt back to hand a straying bird (a reward of real flesh is offered once the falcon is again safe and secure on the fist) and is vital in the process of training.

It will be obvious from the long social history of falconry, and from the high standing of the falconer in the past, that

LEFT: An adult Peregrine on the wrist. Soon the hood will be removed, and when suitable prey has been flushed, the jesses will be released and the falcon 'cast off' in pursuit.

training birds of prey to hunt from the fist is no easy task. There are some clear physical difficulties: the Mongol tribesmen who used Golden Eagles, flown from the fist at wolves while their owner was on horseback, must have been extremely strong to carry such a bird all day – and expert horsemen into the bargain. More than this, as with training almost any animal, a working relationship must be established based on respect and on the very detailed knowledge that the falconer must have of his bird and its habits. Such relationships, as between humans, have a large element of the 'personal' about them, and it may be that a falconer is at his best either with hawks or with falcons, or just cannot get on with one particular bird. In no sense of the word should birds of prey be regarded as pets, nor should the tasks of owning and training one be entered into lightly.

The essentials of training a falcon are learnt by the would-be falconer from an experienced falconer during an extensive 'apprenticeship': approaching training as a trial-and-error procedure, guide-book in hand, is a recipe for failure. The first phase

Ancient and modern! A Harris's Hawk fitted with the falconer's traditional leather jesses and bells, but also equipped with an essentially 20th century aid, a miniature radio transmitter to help in relocating it if it vanishes from sight.

of training is to get the bird used to new experiences while sitting on the gloved fist, securely held by the jesses. The introductions to these new aspects of life (called 'manning') are taken gently, and the bird is kept confident by feeding with titbits of flesh. Once reasonably placid, the second training phase ('calling off') begins. The bird is encouraged to fly back to food on the fist from steadily increasing distances, but is prevented from escaping by means of a light cord attached to its leg. Such training is most effective if carried out daily just before the routine feeding time, when the bird is anxious for food. As confidence grows between man and bird, and as the bird more readily responds to calls or whistles instructing it to fly to the fist, so the retaining cord ('creance') can be dispensed with. The next step is to use the lure as an imitation quarry: the lure is swung round in a circle attached to a line, and the falcon is encouraged to 'stoop' at it in flight, while hawks may be trained first to attack a lure pulled along the ground. Successful stoops are rewarded with a morsel of flesh.

Once the bird is able to travel on the fist, and well enough trained to respond to the falconer's calls, then it can be taken hunting. Novice birds are first flown at easy target quarry, which lack the speed to escape or the flight agility to dodge the attacks easily. Falcons may be flown straight at game off the fist, but more commonly are used in conjunction with a dog. This is falconry at its most spectacular, in the wide-open wild spaces of plains or moors. The dog ranges widely ahead of the falconer, and once it has found likely prey, freezes in the 'point' position indicating where the prey (often grouse or partridge) sits hidden, relying on its camouflage. The falconer casts off his bird, which spirals up overhead to gain height, where she 'waits on' until the falconer disturbs the quarry, putting it up downwind of the waiting falcon. Once the falcon sights quarry, it sets off after it in that fearsome power-dive or stoop, binding on to it in mid-air and forcing it to the ground, usually already dead. On the ground, the falcon half-

extends its wings in a protective 'mantle' over the prey, and may begin to pluck at it, before the falconer gently retrieves the prey and encourages the falcon back onto the glove, rewarding it with a morsel of flesh. The pursuit may involve several stages, with the quarry either seeking shelter or dodging the stoop before the falcon climbs to try again.

Hawks – short wings – are built for quick acceleration, and short high-speed chases where the manoeuvrability conferred by their fingered, rounded wings can be used to best advantage. Thus they are used for hunting in scrub or wooded country, and are flown off the fist ('let slip') as soon as potential quarry is seen. Once a hawk has captured its quarry, the falconer retrieves it and rewards the hawk as he takes its jesses in hand and settles it on his gloved fist.

Today, possibly as yet another reflection of the affluent times in which we live, falconry is taking on a new lease of life and increasing in popularity in many quarters of the globe. Not all those who enthuse over falconry are necessarily involved in the 'thrill of the chase' which inevitably must end in bloodshed and in tragedy for the quarry. Red though nature is in tooth and claw, the participation of man in this killing process cannot be denied, and there are those who quite justly would prefer not to be involved, no matter how stirring the sight of a falcon stooping onto its prey may be. For them, the demonstrations of falconry skills now widely available at 'falconry centres', where birds are flown only to the fist or the lure, are an adequate way of displaying the physique and flight prowess of the birds of prey.

Interestingly, too, in this age of modern technology, falcons have been called on to help protect their man-made equivalents, the jet-engined fighter-bombers of our air forces. Jet engines necessarily use large quantities of air in their combustion processes to produce propulsive thrust, and gathering this air, act like giant vacuum cleaners as they move along the runway. Thus there is a real risk that flocks of birds, ranging in size from Starlings, through Lapwings to gulls, all regular frequenters of the wide open spaces of airfields, may be ingested by the engine, causing not only costly damage but also risking a crash and consequent loss of life. Strive though he may, man has yet to devise a 'scare-crow' with any long-lasting effect, but on airfields a falconer flying his charges at the flocks of birds has been shown to be extremely effective in keeping the runways and their vicinity clear at times of major aircraft movements. Just the presence of the falcon is enough to scare off potentially hazardous species – there seems little need for a kill – so several particularly risk-prone airfields now fly 'squadrons' of falcons, or employ contract falconers, to improve flight safety: yet another intriguing facet to this fascinating group of birds.

Man and bird a picture of elegance: an elderly Pakistani falconer with a Goshawk on his fist.

Holding station over the reeds, a Florida Snail Kite seeks its prey. A remarkably slim, long and sharply-pointed beak, curved into a semicircle, assists in extracting the snail from its shell.

7

THE BIRDS OF PREY
OF THE WORLD
AND THEIR DISTRIBUTION

This list of the birds of prey, their common and their scientific names, has been adapted from a variety of sources. Because taxonomy and classification are essentially dynamic sciences, and because the opinions of museum authorities and other experts may differ, differences may be found between this list and others, and indeed also between those others. The families (e.g. Cathartidae) are arranged in a generally accepted order, but within each family, the genera are arranged in alphabetical sequence for easier reference (for example to discover geographical distribution): thus *Cathartes* precedes *Coragyps*. Likewise, within each genus, the species are listed alphabetically: thus *Cathartes aura* precedes *Cathartes burrovianus*.

CATHARTIDAE · NEW WORLD VULTURES

Cathartes aura	Turkey Vulture	N. & S. America
Cathartes burrovianus	Lesser Yellow-headed Vulture	S. & Central America
Cathartes melambrotus	Greater Yellow-headed Vulture	S. America
Coragyps atratus	Black Vulture	N. & S. America
Sarcorhamphus papa	King Vulture	N. & S. America
Vultur californianus	California Condor	N. & Central America
Vultur gryphus	Andean Condor	S. America

SAGITTARIIDAE · SECRETARY BIRD

Sagittarius serpentarius	Secretary Bird	Africa

ACCIPITRIDAE · HAWKS, OLD WORLD VULTURES, HARRIERS, KITES, EAGLES and BUZZARDS

Accipiter albogularis	Pied Hawk	Australasia
Accipiter badius	Shikra	Africa, Eurasia, S.E. Asia
Accipiter bicolor	Bicolored Hawk	S. & Central America
Accipiter brachyurus	New Britain Sparrowhawk	Australasia
Accipiter brevipes	Levant Sparrowhawk	Eurasia, Africa
Accipiter buergersi	Buerger's Goshawk	Australasia
Accipiter castanilius	Chestnut-flanked Goshawk	Africa
Accipiter cirrocephalus	Collared Sparrowhawk	Australasia
Accipiter collaris	Semicollared Hawk	S. America
Accipiter cooperii	Cooper's Hawk	N. & Central America
Accipiter eichhorni	Imitator Hawk	Australasia
Accipiter erythropus	Red-thighed Sparrowhawk	Africa
Accipiter fasciatus	Brown Goshawk	Australasia
Accipiter francesii	Madagascar Goshawk	Madagascar
Accipiter gentilis	Goshawk	N. America, Eurasia
Accipiter griseiceps	Celebes Crested Goshawk	S.E. Asia
Accipiter gularis	Japanese Sparrowhawk	Asia
Accipiter gundlachi	Gundlach's Hawk	Central America
Accipiter haplochrous	White-bellied Hawk	Australasia

Accipiter henicogrammus	Gray's Goshawk	S.E. Asia
Accipiter hensti	Henst's Goshawk	Africa
Accipiter luteoschistaceus	Blue-and-Gray Sparrowhawk	Australasia
Accipiter madagascariensis	Madagascar Sparrowhawk	Madagascar
Accipiter melanochlamys	Black-mantled Goshawk	Australasia
Accipiter melanoleucus	Great Sparrowhawk	Africa
Accipiter meyerianus	Meyer's Goshawk	Australasia
Accipiter minullus	African Little Sparrowhawk	Africa
Accipiter nisus	Sparrowhawk	Eurasia, S.E. Asia, Africa
Accipiter novaehollandiae	Grey Goshawk	Australasia
Accipiter ovampensis	Ovampo Sparrowhawk	Africa
Accipiter poliocephalus	New Guinea Grey-headed Goshawk	New Guinea
Accipiter poliogaster	Grey-bellied Hawk	S. America
Accipiter princeps	New Britain Grey-headed Goshawk	Australasia
Accipiter rhodogaster	Vinous-breasted Sparrowhawk	S.E. Asia
Accipiter rufitorques	Fiji Goshawk	Fiji
Accipiter rufiventris	Rufous-breasted Sparrowhawk	Africa
Accipiter soloensis	Chinese Sparrowhawk	Asia
Accipiter striatus	Sharp-shinned Hawk	N. & S. America
Accipiter superciliosus	Tiny Hawk	S. & Central America
Accipiter tachiro	African Goshawk	Africa
Accipiter toussenelii	Vinous-chested Goshawk	Africa
Accipiter trinotatus	Spot-tailed Accipiter	S.E. Asia
Accipiter trivirgatus	Crested Goshawk	S. & S.E. Asia
Accipiter virgatus	Besra Sparrowhawk	Eurasia, S.E. Asia
Aegypius monachus	European Black Vulture	Eurasia, Africa, S. Asia
Aegypius tracheliotus	Lappet-faced Vulture	Eurasia, Africa
Aquila audax	Wedge-tailed Eagle	Australasia
Aquila chrysaetos	Golden Eagle	Northern Hemisphere
Aquila clanga	Spotted Eagle	Eurasia, Africa, S. Asia
Aquila gurneyi	Gurney's Eagle	Australasia
Aquila heliaca	Imperial Eagle	Eurasia, Africa, S. Asia
Aquila pomarina	Lesser Spotted Eagle	Eurasia, Africa, S. Asia
Aquila rapax	Tawny Eagle	Eurasia, Africa, S. Asia
Aquila verreauxii	Verreaux's Eagle	Africa
Aquila wahlbergi	Wahlberg's Eagle	Africa
Aviceda cuculoides	African Cuckoo Falcon	Africa
Aviceda jerdoni	Brown-crested Lizard Hawk	S.E. Asia
Aviceda leuphotes	Black-crested Lizard Hawk	S.E. Asia
Aviceda madagascariensis	Madagascar Cuckoo Falcon	Madagascar
Aviceda subcristata	Crested Lizard Hawk	Australasia
Busarellus nigricollis	Black-collared Hawk	Central & S. America
Butastur indicus	Grey-faced Buzzard Eagle	Eurasia, S.E. Asia
Butastur liventer	Rufous-winged Buzzard Eagle	S.E. Asia
Butastur rufipennis	Grasshopper Buzzard	Africa
Butastur teesa	White-eyed Buzzard Eagle	Eurasia, S.E. Asia
Buteo albicaudatus	White-tailed Hawk	N. & S. America
Buteo albonotatus	Zone-tailed Hawk	N. & S. America
Buteo auguralis	African Red-tailed Buzzard	Africa

Buteo brachypterus	Madagascar Buzzard	Madagascar
Buteo brachyurus	Short-tailed Hawk	N. & S. America
Buteo buteo	Common Buzzard	Eurasia, Africa, S.E. Asia
Buteo galapagoensis	Galapagos Hawk	Galapagos Is.
Buteo hemilasius	Upland Buzzard	Asia
Buteo jamaicensis	Red-tailed Hawk	N. & Central America
Buteo lagopus	Rough-legged Hawk	N. America, Eurasia
Buteo leucorrhous	White-rumped Hawk	S. America
Buteo lineatus	Red-shouldered Hawk	N. & Central America
Buteo magnirostris	Roadside Hawk	S. & Central America
Buteo nitidus	Grey Hawk	N. & S. America
Buteo oreophilus	African Mountain Buzzard	Africa
Buteo platypterus	Broad-winged Hawk	N. & S. America
Buteo poecilochrous	Variable Hawk	S. America
Buteo polyosoma	Red-backed Hawk	S. America
Buteo regalis	Ferruginous Hawk	N. & Central America
Buteo ridgwayi	Ridgway's Hawk	Central America
Buteo rufinus	Long-legged Buzzard	Eurasia, Africa
Buteo rufofuscus	Augur Buzzard	Africa
Buteo solitarius	Hawaiian Hawk	Hawaii
Buteo swainsoni	Swainson's Hawk	N. & S. America
Buteo ventralis	Rufous-tailed Hawk	S. America
Buteogallus aequinoctialis	Rufous Crab Hawk	S. America
Buteogallus anthracinus	Black Hawk	N. & S. America
Buteogallus urubitinga	Great Black Hawk	Central & S. America
Chondrohierax uncinatus	Hook-billed Kite	S. & Central America
Circaetus cinerascens	Smaller Banded Snake Eagle	Africa
Circaetus cinereus	Snake Eagle	Africa
Circaetus fasciolatus	Southern Banded Snake Eagle	Africa
Circaetus gallicus	Short-toed Eagle	Eurasia, Africa, S.E. Asia
Circus aeruginosus	Marsh Harrier	Old World, Australasia
Circus assimilis	Spotted Harrier	Australasia
Circus buffoni	Long-winged Harrier	S. America
Circus cinereus	Cinereous Harrier	S. America
Circus cyaneus	Hen Harrier (Marsh Hawk)	Cosmopolitan except Australasia
Circus macrourus	Pallid Harrier	Eurasia, S.E. Asia, Africa
Circus maurus	Black Harrier	Africa
Circus melanoleucus	Pied Harrier	Asia
Circus pygargus	Montagu's Harrier	Eurasia, Africa
Dryotriorchis spectabilis	Congo Snake Eagle	Central Africa
Elanoides forficatus	Swallow-tailed Kite	N. & S. America
Elanus caeruleus	Black-winged Kite	Eurasia, Africa, S.E. Asia, Australasia
Elanus leucurus	White-tailed Kite	N. & S. America
Elanus notatus	Black-shouldered Kite	Australasia
Elanus riocourii	African Swallow-tailed Kite	Africa
Elanus scriptus	Letter-winged Kite	Australasia
Erythrotriorchis radiatus	Red Goshawk	Australasia
Eutriorchis astur	Madagascar Serpent Eagle	Madagascar
Gampsonyx swainsonii	Pearl Kite	S. & Central America

Geranoaetus melanoleucus	Black-chested Buzzard Eagle	S. America
Geranospiza caerulescens	Crane Hawk	S. America
Gypaetus barbatus	Bearded Vulture	Africa, Eurasia, S. Asia
Gypohierax angolensis	Palm-nut Vulture	Africa
Gyps bengalensis	Indian White-backed Vulture	Africa, Eurasia, S. Asia
Gyps coprotheres	Cape Vulture	Africa
Gyps fulvus	Griffon Vulture	Africa, Eurasia
Gyps himalayensis	Himalayan Griffon	Eurasia
Gyps indicus	Long-billed Vulture	S. Asia
Gyps ruppellii	Ruppell's Griffon	Africa
Haliaeetus albicilla	White-tailed Sea Eagle	N. America, Eurasia
Haliaeetus leucocephalus	Bald Eagle	N. America, Eurasia
Haliaeetus leucogaster	White-bellied Sea Eagle	S.E. Asia, Australasia
Haliaeetus leucoryphus	Pallas' Sea Eagle	Eurasia, S.E. Asia
Haliaeetus pelagicus	Steller's Sea Eagle	N. America, Eurasia
Haliaeetus sanfordi	Sanford's Eagle	Australasia
Haliaeetus vocifer	African Fish Eagle	Africa
Haliaeetus vociferoides	Madagascar Fish Eagle	Madagascar
Haliastur indus	Brahminy Kite	S.E. Asia, Australasia
Haliastur sphenurus	Whistling Kite	Australasia
Hamirostra melanosternon	Black-breasted Buzzard	Australasia
Harpagus bidentatus	Double-toothed Kite	S. & Central America
Harpagus diodon	Rufous-thighed Kite	S. America
Harpia harpyia	Harpy Eagle	S. America
Harpyhaliaetus coronatus	Crowned Eagle	S. America
Harpyhaliaetus solitarius	Solitary Eagle	Central & S. America
Harpyopsis novaeguineae	New Guinea Harpy Eagle	New Guinea
Henicopernis infuscata	Black Honey Buzzard	Australasia
Henicopernis longicauda	Long-tailed Buzzard	Australasia
Heterospizias meridionalis	Savanna Hawk	Central & S. America
Hieraaetus dubius	Ayre's Hawk Eagle	Africa
Hieraaetus fasciatus	Bonelli's Eagle	Eurasia, Africa, S. Asia
Hieraaetus kienerii	Rufous-bellied Hawk Eagle	S. & S.E. Asia
Hieraaetus morphnoides	Little Eagle	Australasia
Hieraaetus pennatus	Booted Eagle	Eurasia, Africa, S. Asia
Ichthyophaga ichthyaetus	Grey-headed Fishing Eagle	S.E. Asia
Ichthyophaga nana	Lesser Fishing Eagle	S.E. Asia
Ictinaetus malayensis	Black Eagle	S. & S.E. Asia
Ictinia mississippiensis	Mississippi Kite	N. & S. America
Ictinia plumbea	Plumbeous Kite	S. & Central America
Kaupifalco monogrammicus	Lizard Buzzard	Africa
Leptodon cayanensis	Grey-headed Kite	S. & Central America
Leucopternis albicollis	White Hawk	Central & S. America
Leucopternis kuhli	White-browed Hawk	S. America
Leucopternis lacernulata	White-necked Hawk	S. America
Leucopternis melanops	Black-faced Hawk	S. America
Leucopternis occidentalis	Grey-backed Hawk	S. America
Leucopternis plumbea	Plumbeous Hawk	Central & S. America
Leucopternis polionota	Mantled Hawk	S. America
Leucopternis princeps	Barred Hawk	Central & S. America
Leucopternis schistacea	Slate-colored Hawk	S. America

Leucopternis semiplumbea	Semiplumbeous Hawk	Central & S. America
Lophaetus occipitalis	Long-crested Eagle	Africa
Lophoictinia isura	Square-tailed Kite	Australasia
Macheirhamphus alcinus	Bat Hawk	Africa & S.E. Asia
Megatriorchis doriae	Doria's Hawk	Australasia
Melierax canorus	Pale Chanting Goshawk	Africa
Melierax gabar	Gabar Goshawk	Africa
Melierax metabates	Chanting Goshawk	Africa
Melierax poliopterus	Grey Chanting Goshawk	Africa
Milvus migrans	Black Kite	Old World & Australasia
Milvus milvus	Red Kite	Eurasia, N. Africa
Morphnus guianensis	Crested Eagle	S. America
Neophron monachus	Hooded Vulture	Africa
Neophron percnopterus	Egyptian Vulture	Africa, Eurasia
Oroaetus isidori	Black-and-Chestnut Eagle	S. America
Parabuteo unicinctus	Harris's Hawk	N. & S. America
Pernis apivorus	Honey Buzzard	Eurasia & Africa
Pernis celebensis	Barred Honey Buzzard	S.E. Asia
Pernis ptilorhynchus	Crested Honey Buzzard	Eurasia & S.E. Asia
Pithecophaga jefferyi	Monkey-eating Eagle	S.E. Asia
Polemaetus bellicosus	Martial Eagle	Africa
Polyboroides radiatus	African Harrier Hawk	Africa
Rostrhamus hamatus	Slender-billed Kite	S. America
Rostrhamus sociabilis	Snail Kite	N. & S. America
Sarcogyps calvus	Indian Black Vulture	S. Asia
Spilornis cheela	Crested Serpent Eagle	S. Asia
Spilornis holospilus	Philippine Serpent Eagle	Philippine Is.
Spilornis rufipectus	Celebes Serpent Eagle	S.E. Asia
Spizaetus africanus	Cassin's Hawk Eagle	Africa
Spizaetus alboniger	Blyth's Hawk Eagle	S.E. Asia
Spizaetus bartelsi	Java Hawk Eagle	S.E. Asia
Spizaetus cirrhatus	Crested Hawk Eagle	S. & S.E. Asia
Spizaetus lanceolatus	Celebes Hawk Eagle	S.E. Asia
Spizaetus nanus	Small Hawk Eagle	S.E. Asia
Spizaetus nipalensis	Hodgson's Hawk Eagle	Asia
Spizaetus ornatus	Ornate Hawk Eagle	S. America
Spizaetus philippensis	Philippine Hawk Eagle	Philippine Is.
Spizaetus tyrannus	Black Hawk Eagle	S. & Central America
Spizastur melanoleucus	Black-and-White Hawk Eagle	S. & Central America
Stepanoaetus coronatus	Crowned Eagle	Africa
Terathopius ecaudatus	Bateleur	Africa
Trigonoceps occipitalis	White-headed Vulture	Africa
Urotriorchis macrourus	African Long-tailed Hawk	Africa

PANDIONIDAE · OSPREY

Pandion haliaetus	Osprey	Cosmopolitan

FALCONIDAE · FALCONS, CARACARAS

Daptrius americanus	Red-throated Caracara	S. & Central America
Daptrius ater	Black Caracara	S. America
Falco alopex	Fox Kestrel	Africa
Falco araea	Seychelles Kestrel	Seychelles Is.
Falco ardosiaceus	Grey Kestrel	Africa
Falco berigora	Brown Falcon	Australasia
Falco biarmicus	Lanner Falcon	Eurasia, Africa
Falco cenchroides	Nankeen Kestrel	Australasia
Falco cherrug	Saker Falcon	Eurasia, Africa, S. Asia
Falco chicquera	Red-headed Falcon	Eurasia, Africa, S. Asia
Falco columbarius	Merlin	Cosmopolitan except S.E. Asia & Australasia
Falco concolor	Sooty Falcon	Eurasia, S. Asia, Africa
Falco cuvieri	African Hobby	Africa
Falco deiroleucus	Red-necked Falcon	S. & Central America
Falco dickinsoni	Dickinson's Kestrel	Africa
Falco eleonorae	Eleonora's Falcon	Eurasia, Africa
Falco fasciinucha	Taita Falcon	Africa
Falco femoralis	Aplomado Falcon	N. & S. America
Falco hypoleucus	Grey Falcon	Australasia
Falco jugger	Laggar Falcon	Eurasia, S. Asia
Falco kreyenborgi	Pallid Falcon	S. America
Falco longipennis	Little Falcon	Australasia
Falco mexicanus	Prairie Falcon	N. & Central America
Falco moluccensis	Spotted Kestrel	S.E. Asia
Falco naumanni	Lesser Kestrel	Eurasia, Africa, S. Asia
Falco newtoni	Madagascar Kestrel	Madagascar
Falco novaeseelandiae	New Zealand Falcon	New Zealand
Falco pelegrinoides	Barbary Falcon	Africa
Falco peregrinus	Peregrine Falcon	Cosmopolitan
Falco punctatus	Mauritius Kestrel	Mauritius
Falco rufigularis	Bat Falcon	S. & Central America
Falco rupicoloides	Greater Kestrel	Africa
Falco rusticolus	Gyrfalcon	N. America, Eurasia
Falco severus	Oriental Hobby	S. & S.E. Asia, Australasia
Falco sparverius	American Kestrel	N. & S. America
Falco subbuteo	Hobby	Eurasia, Africa, S. Asia
Falco subniger	Black Falcon	Australasia
Falco tinnunculus	Common Kestrel	Eurasia, Africa, S. Asia
Falco vespertinus	Red-footed Falcon	Eurasia, Africa, S. Asia
Falco zoniventris	Madagascar Banded Kestrel	Madagascar
Herpetotheres cachinnans	Laughing Falcon	S. & Central America
Micrastur buckleyi	Buckley's Forest Falcon	S. America
Micrastur mirandollei	Slaty-backed Forest Falcon	S. & Central America
Micrastur plumbeus	Plumbeous Forest Falcon	S. America
Micrastur ruficollis	Barred Forest Falcon	S. & Central America
Micrastur semitorquatus	Collared Forest Falcon	S. & Central America
Microhierax caerulescens	Red-thighed Falconet	S. & S.E. Asia
Microhierax erythrogonys	Philippine Falconet	Philippine Is.

Microhierax fringillarius	Black-legged Falconet	S.E. Asia
Microhierax latifrons	White-fronted Falconet	S.E. Asia
Microhierax melanoleucos	Pied Falconet	S. Asia
Milvago chimachima	Yellow-headed Caracara	S. & Central America
Milvago chimango	Chimango Caracara	S. America
Phalcoboenus albogularis	White-throated Caracara	S. America
Phalcoboenus australis	Striated Caracara	S. America
Phalcoboenus carunculatus	Carunculated Caracara	S. America
Phalcoboenus megalopterus	Mountain Caracara	S. America
Polihierax insignis	Feilden's Falconet	S. Asia
Polihierax semitorquatus	African Pygmy Falcon	Africa
Polyborus plancus	Crested Caracara	N., Central & S. America
Spiziapteryx circumcinctus	Spot-winged Falconet	S. America

FURTHER READING

So copious is the literature on birds of prey that any selection of suggestions for further, more detailed, reading must inevitably leave out a number of major works. Also, the nature of any further reading must to a large degree be a matter of personal choice, depending upon whether it is ecology, field identification, falconry, conservation or detailed species biology that is to be the subject of further investigation.

The selection of books that follows aims to cover many of the topics outlined in the preceding chapters, and in each, ample further references may be located, particularly to papers published in scientific journals. Almost all countries across the world now have compact, well-illustrated field guides to their birds, and although, with the wide variety of immature plumages, especially among the larger species, the birds of prey are not ideally covered in many such guides, all are an invaluable starting point. They are equally useful to the resident in and the newcomer to an area.

One two-volume work stands out above all others as a comprehensive guide to all the birds of prey of the World: their distribution, biology and ecology, and plumages. This is the two-volume:

Eagles, Hawks and Falcons of the World, by Leslie Brown and Dean Amadon, published in 1968 by Collins, London.

Similarly comprehensive but more limited in geographical or taxonomic scope, are the:

Handbook of Birds of Europe, the Middle East and North Africa, Volume 2, edited by Stanley Cramp, published in 1982 by the Oxford University Press, Oxford.

Birds of Africa, Volume 1, by Leslie Brown, Emil K Urban and Kenneth Newman, published in 1982 by Academic Press, London and New York.

Falcons of the World, by Tom J Cade, published in 1982 by Collins, London. This contains much detailed information on falcons, and valuable sections on falconry and on conservation.

Bird of prey ecology is dealt with admirably in *Population Ecology of Raptors*, by Ian Newton, published in 1979 by T and A D Poyser, Calton.

An excellent guide, which deals with the intricacies and difficulties of identifying birds of prey, both thoroughly and practically, is *Flight Identification of European Raptors*, by R F Porter, Ian Willis, Steen Christensen and Bent Pors Nielsen (third edition 1981) published by T and A D Poyser, Calton.

Three of the best individual species studies to appear recently have also been published by T and A D Poyser. They are:

The Hen Harrier, by Donald Watson (1977)

The Peregrine Falcon, by Derek Ratcliffe (1980)

The Sparrowhawk, by Ian Newton (1986).

INDEX

Page numbers in *italic* refer to the illustrations

Accipiter, 52, 68
Accipiter striatus, 58
Accipitridae, 11, 47–119, 125, 127, 166–70
Africa, 46, 49, 123, 130, 131
African Cuckoo Falcon (*Aviceda cuculoides*), 167
African Fish Eagle (*Haliaeetus vocifer*), 11, 12, 22, 106–8, *106*, *108*, 169
African Goshawk (*Accipiter tachiro*), *54*, 167
African Harrier Hawk (*Polyboroides radiatus*), *56*, 170
African Hawk Eagle see Bonelli's Eagle
African Hobby (*Falco cuvieri*), 171
African Little Sparrowhawk (*Accipiter minullus*), *54*, 167
African Long-tailed Hawk (*Urotriorchis macrourus*), 170
African Mountain Buzzard (*Buteo oreophilus*), 168
African Pygmy Falconet (*Polihierax semitorquatus*), 172
African Red-tailed Buzzard (*Buteo auguralis*), 167
African Rift Valley, 37
African Swallow-tailed Kite (*Elanus riocourii*), 168
air-sacs, 29
Alaska, 34, 99, 102, 105
Amazonia, 82
American Kestrel (*Falco sparverius*), *125*, 171
Andean Condor (*Vultur gryphus*), *18*, 27, 32, 43, *43*, 166
Antarctica, 120
Aplomado Falcon (*Falco femoralis*), 171
Aquila, 82, 89–90
Arabia, 130
Arctic, 32, 34
Argentina, 78
Arkaig, Loch, *123*
Asia, 58, 123, 130, 141, 158
Assyria, 158
Augur Buzzard (*Buteo rufofuscus*), *68*, 168
Australia, 49, 120, 131, 140–5
Australian Goshawk see Brown Goshawk
Australian Kestrel (*Falco cenchroides*), 131
Ayre's Hawk Eagle (*Hieraaetus dubius*), 169
Bald Eagle (*Haliaeetus leucocephalus*), 22, *40*, 79, 99–105, *100–4*, 169
Baltic, 37
Barbary Falcon (*Falco pelegrinoides*), 171

Barn Owl (*Tyto alba*), *10*
Barred Forest Falcon (*Micrastur ruficollis*), 171
Barred Hawk (*Leucopternis princeps*), 169
Barred Honey Buzzard (*Pernis celebensis*), 170
Bat-eating Buzzard see Bat Hawk
Bat Falcon (*Falco rufigularis*), 11, 171
Bat Hawk (*Macheirhamphus alcinus*), 49, 170
Bateleur Eagle (*Terathopius ecaudatus*), *38*, *83*, 88, 170
bathing, 15
Bayeux Tapestry, 158
bazas, 49
beaks, 20, *20–3*
Bearded Vulture (Lammergeier, *Gypaetus barbatus*), 112, *114*, 119, *153*, 169
Besra Sparrowhawk (*Accipiter virgatus*), 167
Bicolored Hawk (*Accipiter bicolor*), 166
Black-and-Chestnut Eagle (*Oroaetus isidori*), 170
Black-and-White Hawk Eagle (*Spizastur melanoleucus*), 170
Black-breasted Buzzard (*Hamirostra melanosternon*), 142, 169
Black Caracara (*Daptrius ater*), 171
Black-chested Buzzard Eagle (*Geranoaetus melanoleucus*), *86*, 169
Black-collared Fishing Hawk (*Busarellus nigricollis*), 78, 167
Black-crested Lizard Hawk (*Aviceda leuphotes*), 167
Black Eagle (*Ictinaetus malayensis*), 89–92, 169
Black-faced Hawk (*Leucopternis melanops*), 169
Black Falcon (*Falco subniger*), *140*, 142, 145, 171
Black Harrier (*Circus maurus*), 168
Black Hawk Eagle (*Spizaetus tyrannus*), 170
Black Honey Buzzard (*Henicopernis infuscata*), 169
Black Kite (*Milvus migrans*), *30*, 47, *48*, 49, *50*, *119*, 170
Black-legged Falconet (*Microhierax fringillarius*), 172
Black-mantled Goshawk (*Accipiter melanochlamys*), 167
Black-shouldered Kite (*Elanus notatus*), *22*, 48, 142, *142*, 168
Black Sparrowhawk see Great Sparrowhawk
Black Vulture (*Coragyps atratus*), *12*, *19*, 43, *44*, *119*, 166
Black-winged Kite (*Elanus caeruleus*), 168
blood supply, 29
Blue-and-Grey Sparrowhawk (*Accipiter luteoschistaceus*), 167
Blyth's Hawk Eagle (*Spizaetus

alboniger*), *82*, 170
Boke of St Albans, 158
Bonelli's Eagle (*Hieraaetus fasciatus*), *82*, *90*, *149*, *156*, 169
bones, 18–19
Booted Eagle (*Hieraaetus pennatus*), *89*, 169
booted eagles, 87–92
Bosphorus, 37
Brahminy Kite (*Haliastur indus*), *49*, *143*, 169
breeding, 38–9
Britain, 123, 151, 158
Broad-winged Hawk (*Buteo platypterus*), 168
Brown Falcon (*Falco berigora*), *143*, 145, 171
Brown Goshawk (*Accipiter fasciatus*), *143*, 144, 166
Brown-crested Lizard Hawk (*Aviceda jerdoni*), 167
Buckley's Forest Falcon (*Micrastur buckleyi*), 171
Buerger's Goshawk (*Accipiter buergersi*), 166
Buteo, 32, 52, 68–70
Buteoninae, 68
buzzards, 12, *13*, 37, 68–78, 96, 98

California Condor (*Vultur californianus*), 43, *43*, 166
Canada, 34, 102, 105
Canary Islands, 131
Cape Vulture (*Gyps coprotheres*), *112*, 169
caracaras, 29, 125–9
carrion, 27
Carunculated Caracara (*Phalcoboenus carunculatus*), 172
Cassin's Hawk Eagle (*Spizaetus africanus*), 170
Cathartidae, 43, 166
Celebes Crested Goshawk (*Accipiter griseiceps*), 166
Celebes Hawk Eagle (*Spizaetus lanceolatus*), 170
Celebes Serpent Eagle (*Spilornis rufipectus*), 170
Central America, 70
Changeable Hawk Eagle see Crested Hawk Eagle
Chanting Goshawk (*Melierax metabates*), 52, *56*, 170
Chestnut-flanked Goshawk (*Accipiter castanilius*), 166
Chimango Caracara (*Milvago chimango*), 172
China, 158
Chinese Sparrowhawk (*Accipiter soloensis*), 167
Cinereous Harrier (*Circus cinereus*), 168
Circus, 32, 63
clutch sizes, 38
Collared Forest Falcon (*Micrastur semitorquatus*), 171

Collared Sparrowhawk (*Accipiter cirrocephalus*), 144, 166
Common Black Hawk (*Buteogallus anthracinus*), 78, 168
Common Buzzard (*Buteo buteo*), 27, 70, *72*, 78, 129, 168
condors, 10
Congo Snake Eagle (*Dryotriorchis spectabilis*), 168
conservation, 148–55
Cooper's Hawk (*Accipiter cooperii*), *55*, 166
Cotapaxi, 32
courtship displays, 15, 39
Crane Hawk (*Geranospiza caerulescens*), 169
Crested Caracara (*Polyborus plancus*), *128*, 172
Crested Eagle (*Morphnus guianensis*), 170
Crested Goshawk (*Accipiter trivirgatus*), 167
Crested Hawk Eagle (*Spizaetus cirrhatus*), *84*, 170
Crested Honey Buzzard (*Pernis ptilorhynchus*), *51*, 170
Crested Lizard Hawk (*Aviceda subcristata*), 143, 167
Crested Serpent Eagle (*Spilornis cheela*), *91*, 170
Crowned Eagle, (*Harpyhaliaetus coronatus*), 169
Crowned Eagle (*Stephanoaetus coronatus*), *29*, 170
cuckoo-falcons, 49

DDT, 154–5
Dickinson's Kestrel (*Falco dickinsoni*), 171
diet, 10, 27 see also feeding
display flights, 39
Doria's Hawk (*Megatriorchis doriae*), 170
Double-toothed Kite (*Harpagus bidentatus*), 169

eagles, 21, 37, 38, 79–93
ears, 25
egg collecting, 150–1
eggs, 38, *151*
Egypt, 131
Egyptian Vulture (*Neophron percnopterus*), 110, 112, *112*, *119*, 170
Eilat, 37
Eleonora's Falcon (*Falco eleonorae*), 38, 171
Eurasia, 135
Europe, 58, 123, 130, 137, 151, 158
European Black Vulture (*Aegypius monachus*), 167
Everest, Mount, 32
eyesight, 25–7

Falco, 32, 130
Falconidae, 125–40, 171–2
Falconinae, 129–30

falconry, 151, *156*, 158–63, *159–61, 163*
falcons, 125–40, 145
  beaks, 20
  display flights, 39
  falconry, 158, 159, 162
  nests, 38
  wing, 22
Falkland Islands, 128
Falsterbo, 37
feathers, 15
feeding, 15, 39 *see also* diet
feet, 18–20, *18, 19*, 22, *25*
Feilden's Falconet (*Polihierax insignis*), 172
female birds, size, 27–9
Ferruginous Hawk (*Buteo regalis*), 168
Fiji Goshawk (*Accipiter rufitorques*), 167
fish, catching, 22
fish eagles, 32, 112
fledglings, 39
Florida, 105
flying, 18
  display flights, 39
food dropping, 39, 63
Fox Kestrel (*Falco alopex*), 171

Gabar Goshawk (*Melierax gabar*), *54*, 170
Galapagos Hawk (*Buteo galapagoensis*), *70, 78*, 168
gamekeepers, 148, *148*
Germany, 158
gibbets, 148, *148*
Gibraltar, 37
Golden Eagle (*Aquila chrysaetos*), 11, *19*, 82, 89, 96–9, *96, 97, 98*, 155, 158, 161, 167
Goshawk (*Accipiter gentilis*), 21, 52, *53, 54*, 60, *151*, 158, *163*, 166
Grasshopper Buzzard (*Butastur rufipennis*), *74*, 167
Grey-backed Hawk (*Leucopternis occidentalis*), 169
Grey-bellied Hawk (*Accipiter poliogaster*), 167
Grey Chanting Goshawk (*Melierax poliopterus*), 170
Grey-faced Buzzard Eagle (*Butastur indicus*), 167
Grey Falcon (*Falco hypoleucus*), 142, 145, 171
Grey Goshawk (*Accipiter novaehollandiae*), 143, 167
Grey Hawk (*Buteo nitidus*), 168
Grey-headed Fishing Eagle (*Ichthyophaga ichthyaetus*), 169
Grey-headed Kite (*Leptodon cayanensis*), 169
Grey Kestrel (*Falco ardosiaceus*), 171
Gray's Goshawk (*Accipiter henicogrammus*), 167
Great Black Hawk (*Buteogallus urubitinga*), 78, 168

Great Sparrowhawk (*Accipiter melanoleucus*), *58*, 167
Greater Kestrel (*Falco rupicoloides*), 171
Greater Yellow-headed Vulture (*Cathartes melambrotus*), 166
Griffon Vulture (*Gyps fulvus*), 114, *118*, 119, 169
Gundlach's Hawk (*Accipiter gundlachi*), 166
Gurney's Eagle (*Aquila gurneyi*), 167
Gyrfalcon (*Falco rusticolus*), 32, *33*, 128, 158, 171

habitat, 32
Haliaeetus, 32
Harpy Eagle (*Harpia harpyia*), 82–3, 88–9, *88*, 169
harriers, 21–2, 63, 145
Harris's Hawk (*Parabuteo unicinctus*), *75, 161*, 170
Hawaiian Hawk (*Buteo solitarius*), 168
hawk-eagles, 88
Hawk Mountain, 37, 150
hawk-shoots, 150
hawks, 12, 52, 127
  falconry, 158, 159, 162
  migration, 37
  tails, 21
hearing, 25
heart, 29
Hen Harrier *see* Marsh Hawk
Henicopernis, 51–2
Henst's Goshawk (*Accipiter hensti*), 167
Herpetotheres, 128
Herpetotherinae, 128
Himalayan Griffon Vulture (*Gyps himalayensis*), 32, 169
Hobby (*Falco subbuteo*), 22–4, *127*, 158, 171
Hodgson's Hawk Eagle (*Spizaetus nipalensis*), *82*, 170
Holland, 133–5
Honey Buzzard (*Pernis apivorus*), 51–2, *52*, 170
Hooded Vulture (*Neophron monachus*), *8*, 112, *113*, 170
Hook-billed Kite (*Chondrohierax uncinatus*), 51, 168
hovering, 22, *22*, 25, 131–2
hunting techniques, 21–7

Imitator Hawk (*Accipiter eichhorni*), 166
Imperial Eagle (*Aquila heliaca*), 20, *83*, 167
Indian Black Vulture (*Sarcogyps calvus*), *112*, 170
Indian White-backed Vulture (*Gyps bengalensis*), *112*, 114, 169
Israel, 37

Japan, 158
Japanese Sparrowhawk (*Accipiter gularis*), 166

Java Hawk Eagle (*Spizaetus bartelsi*), 170
Jay, 60, 133, 148
Judean desert, *35*
jungle, *37*, 152

Kearton, Cherry, *123*
Kestrel (*Falco tinnunculus*), *2*, 22, 25–7, *32*, 38, 130–5, *131–3*, 145, 152, 171
King Vulture (*Sarcorhamphus papa*), *44*, 166
kites, 47–9, 51, 83, 143

Laggar Falcon (*Falco jugger*), *125*, 171
Lammergeier *see* Bearded Vulture
Lanner Falcon (*Falco biarmicus*), *16, 35, 130*, 158, 159, 171
Lappet-faced Vulture (*Aegypius tracheliotus*), *10*, *118*, 167
Laughing Falcon (*Herpetotheres cachinnans*), 128, *130*, 171
legs, 18–20
Lesser Fishing Eagle (*Ichthyophaga nana*), 169
Lesser Kestrel (*Falco naumanni*), *128*, 171
Lesser Spotted Eagle (*Aquila pomarina*), *94*, 167
Lesser Yellow-headed Vulture (*Cathartes burrovianus*), *43*, 166
Letter-winged Kite (*Elanus scriptus*), 142, 168
Levant Sparrowhawk (*Accipiter brevipes*), 166
life-span, 15
Little Eagle (*Hieraaetus morphnoides*), 144, *144*, 169
Little Falcon (*Falco longipennis*), *145, 171*
Lizard Buzzard (*Kaupifalco monogrammicus*), *70*, 169
Long-billed Vulture (*Gyps indicus*), 169
Long-crested Hawk Eagle (*Lophaetus occipitalis*), *91*, 170
Long-legged Buzzard (*Buteo rufinus*), 168
Long-tailed Buzzard (*Henicopernis longicauda*), 169
Long-winged Harrier (*Circus buffoni*), 168

Madagascar Banded Kestrel (*Falco zoniventris*), 171
Madagascar Buzzard (*Buteo brachypterus*), 168
Madagascar Cuckoo Falcon (*Aviceda madagascariensis*), 167
Madagascar Fish Eagle (*Haliaeetus vociferoides*), 169
Madagascar Goshawk (*Accipiter francesii*), 166
Madagascar Kestrel (*Falco newtoni*), 171
Madagascar Serpent Eagle (*Eutriorchis astur*), 168
Madagascar Sparrowhawk

(*Accipiter madagascariensis*), 167
Magpie (*Pica pica*), 133, 148
male birds, size, 27–9
Mantled Hawk (*Leucopternis polionota*), 169
Marsh Harrier (*Circus aeruginosus*), 20, *67*, 168
Marsh Hawk (Hen Harrier, *Circus cyaneus*), *64, 65*, 168
Marsupials, 140
Martial Eagle (*Polemaetus bellicosus*), *94*, 170
Mauritius Kestrel (*Falco punctatus*), 171
Mediterranean, 37, 123
Merlin (*Falco columbarius*), 24, *127*, 158, 159, 171
Mexico, 70, 78, 82
Meyer's Goshawk (*Accipiter meyerianus*), 167
Micrastur, 128
Middle East, 158
migration, 34–7
Mississippi Kite (*Ictinia mississippiensis*), 169
Moluccan Kestrel (*Falco moluccensis*), 131
Mongolia, 158, 161
Monkey-eating Eagle (*Pithecophaga jefferyi*), *84*, 170
Montagu's Harrier (*Circus pygargus*), *64, 67*, 168
Mountain Caracara (*Phalcoboenus megalopterus*), 172
Mountain Hawk Eagle *see* Hodgson's Hawk Eagle

names, scientific, 12
Nankeen Kestrel (*Falco cenchroides*), *145, 145*, 171
nests, 37–8
New Britain Grey-headed Goshawk (*Accipiter princeps*), 167
New Britain Sparrowhawk (*Accipiter brachyurus*), 166
New Guinea, 87, 142
New Guinea Grey-headed Goshawk (*Accipiter poliocephalus*), 167
New Guinea Harpy Eagle (*Harpyopsis novaeguineae*), 169
New World Vultures, 43
New Zealand Falcon (*Falco novaeseelandiae*), *141*, 171
North America, 38, 43, 49, 58, 78, 99–105, 120, 131, 135, 137

Old World vultures, 108–19
Oriental Hobby (*Falco severus*), 171
Ornate Hawk Eagle (*Spizaetus ornatus*), 170
Osprey (*Pandion haliaetus*), *4*, 22, *22*, 32, 38, 99, 106, 108, 120–3, *121–3*, 141, 145, *151*, 170
Ovampo Sparrowhawk (*Accipiter ovampensis*), 167
owls, 11, 24–5, 127

Palaearctic, 58, 60
Pale Chanting Goshawk (*Melierax canorus*), *54*, 170
Pallas' Sea Eagle (*Haliaeetus leucoryphus*), *80*, 169
Pallid Falcon (*Falco kreyenborgi*), 171
Pallid Harrier (*Circus macrourus*), 168
Palm-nut Vulture (*Gypohierax angolensis*), 27, *27*, *110*, 111–12, 169
Pandionidae, 120–3, 170
Pearl Kite (*Gampsonyx swainsonii*), *168*
pecten, 27
pellets, 27
Pennsylvania, 150
Peregrine Falcon (*Falco peregrinus*), 24, *25*, 32, *37*, 96, 98, 120, 128, 130, 135–40, *135–9*, 141, 145, 151, *151*, 155, 158, 159, *159*, *161*, 171
Perninae, 51
Pernis, 51–2
pesticides, 105, 140, 152–5
Philippine Pygmy Falconet (*Microhierax erythrogonys*), 129, 172
Philippine Hawk Eagle (*Spizaetus philippensis*), 170
Philippine Serpent Eagle (*Spilornis holospilus*), 170
Philippines, 87, 129
Pied Falconet (*Microhierax melanoleucos*), 172
Pied Harrier (*Circus melanoleucos*), 168
Pied Hawk (*Accipiter albogularis*), 166
'plucking posts', 61–3
Plumbeous Forest Falcon (*Micrastur plumbeus*), 171
Plumbeous Hawk (*Leucopternis plumbea*), 169
Plumbeous Kite (*Ictinia plumbea*), 169
pole traps, *148*
Pondicherri Vulture *see* Indian Black Vulture
Prairie Falcon (*Falco mexicanus*), *127*, 171
preening, 15
pygmy falcons, *10*, 129–30

Ratcliffe, Dr Derek, 155
Raven (*Corvus corax*), 96, 98, *119*, 135
Red-backed Buzzard (*Buteo polyosoma*), 69, 168
Red-footed Falcon (*Falco vespertinus*), 22–4, *24*, 171
Red Goshawk (*Erythrotriorchis radiatus*), 142, *143*, 168
Red-headed Falcon (*Falco chicquera*), 171
Red Kite (*Milvus milvus*), 47, *49*, 170
Red-necked Falcon (*Falco

deiroleucus*), *125*, 171
Red Sea, 37
Red-shouldered Hawk (*Buteo lineatus*), 44, *76*, 168
Red-tailed Buzzard (*Buteo jamaicensis*), 69, 168
Red-thighed Falconet (*Microhierax caerulescens*), *128*, 171
Red-thighed Sparrowhawk (*Accipiter erythropus*), 166
Red-throated Caracara (*Daptrius americanus*), 171
respiratory system, 29
Ridgway's Hawk (*Buteo ridgwayi*), 168
Roadside Hawk (*Buteo magnirostris*), 70, 168
Rought-legged Buzzard (*Buteo lagopus*), 19, *72*, *151*, 168
Rufous-bellied Hawk Eagle (*Hieraaetus kienerii*), 169
Rufous-breasted Sparrowhawk (*Accipiter rufiventris*), 167
Rufous Crab Hawk (*Buteogallus aequinoctialis*), 78, 168
Rufous-tailed Hawk (*Buteo ventralis*), 168
Rufous-thighed Kite (*Harpagus diodon*), 169
Rufous-winged Buzzard Eagle (*Butastur liventer*), 167
Ruppell's Griffon Vulture (*Gyps ruppellii*), *113*, *116*, 169
Russia, 34, 37, 58

Sagittariidae, 46–7, 166
Saker Falcon (*Falco cherrug*), 23, *35*, *158*, 159, 171
Sanford's Eagle (*Haliaeetus sanfordi*), 169
Saudi Arabia, 158
Savanna Hawk (*Heterospizias meridionalis*), 169
scientific names, 12
Scotland, 123
sea crossings, 37
sea eagles, 83, 99
Second World War, 138–40
Secretary Bird (*Sagittarius serpentarius*), 18, 46–7, *46*, *47*, 166
Semicollared Hawk (*Accipiter collaris*), 166
Semiplumbeous Hawk (*Leucopternis semiplumbea*), 170
Seychelles Kestrel (*Falco araea*), 171
Sharp-shinned Hawk (*Accipiter striatus*), 52, 167
Shikra (*Accipiter badius*), *56*, 166
Short-tailed Hawk (*Buteo brachyurus*), 168
Short-toed Eagle (*Circaetus gallicus*), *21*, 79, 88, *88*, 168
size, 27–9
skeleton, 18–9
Slate-colored Hawk (*Leucopternis schistacea*), 169

Slaty-backed Forest Falcon (*Micrastur mirandollei*), 171
Slender-billed Kite (*Rostrhamus hamatus*), 170
Small Hawk Eagle (*Spizaetus nanus*), 170
Smaller Banded Snake Eagle (*Circaetus cinerascens*), 168
Snail Kite (*Rostrhamus sociabilis*), 49, *164*, 170
snake-eagles, 88
Snake Eagle (*Circaetus cinereus*), 79, *86*, 168
Snake Falcon *see* Laughing Falcon
snakes, as prey, 29, 46
Solitary Eagle (*Harpyhaliaetus solitarius*), 169
Sooty Falcon (*Falco concolor*), 171
South America, 32, 43, 49, 78, 120, 129, 130
South-east Asia, 49, 130, 131
Southern Banded Snake Eagle (*Circaetus fasciolatus*), 168
Sparrowhawk (*Accipiter nisus*), 27, 52, *54*, 58–63, *59–63*, *152*, *154*, 158, 167
Sparrowhawk (*Falco sparverius*), 131
species, 11–12
Spilornis, 88
sport, 150, 151, 158–63
Spot-tailed Accipiter (*Accipiter trinotatus*), 167
Spot-winged Falconet (*Spiziapteryx circumcinctus*), 172
Spotted Eagle (*Aquila clanga*), 89, 167
Spotted Harrier (*Circus assimilis*), 145, 168
Spotted Kestrel (*Falco moluccensis*), 171
Square-tailed Kite (*Lophoictinia isura*), 142, 170
Steller's Sea Eagle (*Haliaeetus pelagicus*), 169
Steppe Buzzard, *79*
Steppe Eagle, *86*, 89
stooping, 24, 130, 135–7
Striated Caracara (*Phalcoboenus australis*), *128*, 172
stuffed birds, 150, *150*
Swainson's Hawk (*Buteo swainsoni*), *168*
Swallow-tailed Kite (Elanoides forficatus), 51, 168
Sweden, 37
Swift (*Apus apus*), 12, 22

tails, 21
Taita Falcon (*Falco fasciinucha*), 171
talons, *18*, *19*, *20*, *25*
Tawny Eagle (*Aquila rapax*), 89, *92*, *152*, 167
taxidermy, 150, *150*
Teratornis incredibilis, 43
terminology, 12
territorial displays, 15, 39
thermals, 15, 35, 37, 110

Tiny Hawk (*Accipiter superciliosus*), 167
tundra, 32, 34
Turkey Vulture (*Cathartes aura*), 43, *44*, 166

United States of America, 37, 99, 122, 128, 151, 158
Upland Buzzard (*Buteo hemilasius*), 168

Vanuatu, 142
Variable Hawk (*Buteo poecilochrous*), 168
Verreaux's Eagle (*Aquila verreauxii*), *87*, 89, 167
Vinous-breasted Sparrowhawk (*Accipiter rhodogaster*), 167
Vinous-chested Goshawk (*Accipiter toussenelii*), 167
vultures, 10, 18, 21, 29, *108*
  New World Vultures, 43
  Old World Vultures, 108–19
Vulturine Fish Eagle *see* Palm-nut Vulture

Wahlberg's Eagle (*Aquila wahlbergi*), *94*, 167
Wedge-tailed Eagle (*Aquila audax*), 89, *140*, 144–5, 167
Whistling Kite (*Haliastur sphenurus*), 169
White-bellied Hawk (*Accipiter haplochrous*), 166
White-bellied Sea Eagle (*Haliaeetus leucogaster*), 79, 80, 141, 145, 169
White-browed Hawk (*Leucopternis kuhli*), 169
White-eyed Buzzard Eagle (*Butastur teesa*), 78, 167
White-fronted Falconet (*Microhierax latifrons*), 172
White Hawk (*Leucopternis albicollis*), 169
White-headed Vulture (*Trigonoceps occipitalis*), *110*, 170
White-necked Hawk (*Leucopternis lacernulata*), 169
White-rumped Hawk (*Buteo leucorrhous*), 168
White-tailed Buzzard (*Buteo albicaudatus*), 70, 167
White-tailed Kite (*Elanus leucurus*), 168
White-tailed Sea Eagle (*Haliaeetus albicilla*), *80*, *146*, 169
White-throated Caracara (*Phalcoboenus albogularis*), 172
wings, 21–2
Woodpigeon (*Columba palumbus*), 52, 60

Yellow-headed Caracara (*Milvago chimachima*), 172
young birds, care of, 15

Zone-tailed Hawk (*Buteo albonotatus*), 167